Advance Praise for

Miracles

AND OTHER
REASONABLE
THINGS

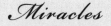

"This book—the fullness, depth, and beauty of Sarah Bessey's faith and artistic genius—is a miracle. Sarah, a prophet who cries out with fury from the pulpit and who whispers tenderly from the page, is simply my favorite faith writer. With *Miracles and Other Reasonable Things* she invites us to lives of wonder by opening our eyes to the ordinary, extraordinary miracles of our days."

—Glennon Doyle, #1 *New York Times* bestselling author of
Untamed and founder of Together Rising

"*Miracles and Other Reasonable Things* will surprise and delight you. Sarah's writing is so breathtaking, sometimes you think you are reading poetry. The story is so thrilling, sometimes you think you are devouring a novel. And the Spirit she describes is so compelling, you'll swear you experienced a revival. You won't put it down once until you close the last page. We are so lucky to be readers in the era of Sarah Bessey."

—Jen Hatmaker, *New York Times* bestselling author of
For the Love and *Of Mess and Moxie* and host of
the podcast *For the Love! with Jen Hatmaker*

"Sarah Bessey is a writer of remarkable gifts. Beyond her ability to make a breathtaking sentence, and to tell the truth about the dying and rising of faith, she can tell a story as if she were whispering it straight into your heart. She is, by her own definition, a dangerous woman, with wisdom to spare about learning to love the broken miracles God offers us once we're honest about where it hurts."

—Barbara Brown Taylor, author of
Learning to Walk in the Dark

"In *Miracles and Other Reasonable Things*, Sarah shows us how pain and loss can teach us to let go of what binds us in our faith stories while clinging to that which helps us survive—and ultimately thrive."

—Mike McHargue, cofounder of The Liturgist Podcast and host of *Ask Science Mike*

"Wise and funny, Sarah Bessey writes with hard-won hope that the space between healed and sick can be sacred ground. Thank God for Sarah, a faithful companion to those of us on the losing side of life."

—Kate Bowler, *New York Times* bestselling author of *Everything Happens for a Reason*

"Sarah Bessey, the self-described introvert, has given us all a witty and intimate personal reflection on faith and life that borders on liturgy. She walks the walk of an evolving faith, with power and vulnerability, guiding us through the common experience of listening to God's nudge (and painful jolt) so we can relearn God again and again, and in so doing witness our own process of unbecoming and rebecoming people of faith. Thank you, Sarah, for putting yourself out there!"

—Peter Enns, author of *How the Bible Actually Works*

"Sarah Bessey's *Miracles and Other Reasonable Things* is immediately one of my favorite books. I can't think of a single other work that brings together such raw, vulnerable pain with such a real sense of enchantment. Sarah is not too pious to tell us the truth about suffering, but not too cool to tell us the truth about the magic either. In this trailblazing, bush-burning book, anything can happen: the Pope shows up, and God does too . . . except of course, when God doesn't."

—Jonathan Martin, author of *How to Survive a Shipwreck* and *Prototype*

"Bessey's moving exploration of how trauma changed and strengthened her relationship with God will appeal to fans of Barbara Brown Taylor."

—*Publishers Weekly*

"Blending theology and memoir, Bessey's latest is a well-written reminder of seeing the miracles in life's highs and lows."

—*Library Journal*

Miracles
AND OTHER
REASONABLE
THINGS

A STORY OF UNLEARNING
AND RELEARNING GOD

SARAH BESSEY

HOWARD BOOKS
—
ATRIA

New York   London   Toronto   Sydney   New Delhi

HOWARD BOOKS
ATRIA

An Imprint of Simon & Schuster, Inc.
1230 Avenue of the Americas
New York, NY 10020

First Howard Books/Atria Paperback edition October 2020

HOWARD BOOKS / ATRIA PAPERBACK and colophon are trademarks of Simon & Schuster, Inc.

For information about special discounts for bulk purchases,
please contact Simon & Schuster Special Sales at 1-866-506-1949
or business@simonandschuster.com.

The Simon & Schuster Speakers Bureau can bring authors to your live event.
For more information or to book an event, contact the Simon & Schuster Speakers Bureau
at 1-866-248-3049 or visit our website at www.simonspeakers.com.

Manufactured in the United States of America

1 3 5 7 9 10 8 6 4 2

Library of Congress Cataloging-in-Publication Data is available.

ISBN 978-1-5011-5546-8
ISBN 978-1-9821-2613-1 (pbk)
ISBN 978-1-5011-5547-5 (ebook)

For my father, K. David Styles.

It wasn't until I wrote the last word of this book that I realized it may actually be a love letter to you. Thank you for the day you told me to "go seek God" with your full blessing— even if my wandering led me out and away from your familiar paths. You were never afraid for me to go, and so I was never afraid of the wilderness. Your love has been our shelter and our home.

Thank you for a lifetime of ordinary miracles.

We're all stories, in the end. Just make it a good one, eh?

—The Doctor

CONTENTS

CONTENTS

PART IV

FOREWORD

I'll just plunge right into the heart of things: Sarah Bessey is one of the best writers writing right now, and this book is Sarah at her best. Frankly, I'm jealous of you because you haven't read it yet.

One of my worst habits is waking up in the night and, instead of just turning over and falling back asleep, reaching for a book and reading till the light breaks across our courtyard onto the red bricks of the chapel next door. When Sarah sent me the manuscript for this beautiful book, it was almost like its presence on my nightstand woke me, whispered to me in the middle of the night—sort of how leftover pizza in the refrigerator also sometimes whispers to me in the night.

The lights of Manhattan outside our window kept me company as I read this book straight through, and I cried when it was over, like saying good-bye to someone I love after having had the pleasure of being on a long journey together, because that's exactly what this book is like: walking shoulder to shoulder through wild terrain, as pilgrims together along the path, borrowing bravery and perspective from your wise companion.

In friendship, if you want to create the kind of space between you that is strong and durable and deeply valuable, you have to be willing to go first. And part of why books matter and writing matters and storytelling matters is because the best writers go first: the best writers say the unsaid and unspoken, the secret truths we all feel but can't quite speak aloud. And in these pages, Sarah's willingness to go first in all sorts of ways is a sacred gift, a permission slip, a key unlocking doors long closed.

So many people in my life are whispering to me right now, almost like a confession, telling me the things they used to believe but don't or can't anymore. These conversations are holy spaces, and I don't take them lightly. Because for many of us, the truth is that we want to stay. We want to be Christians. But the truth is also that there are pieces that no longer fit, and that's scary, or at the very least, sometimes awkward to speak aloud.

What Sarah does so beautifully is create space and safety and permission to crack open our secret hearts and speak plainly about what we're keeping and what we're leaving behind. She draws us close, gives us a safe place to land when our minds and spirits are whirling with anxiety about the unknown places we're entering, these new lands beyond what we used to know and believe.

This beautiful book about miracles is a miracle itself: an honest account of hoping and losing hope, longing and waiting, screwing up the courage to believe again, and finding it tremendously worthwhile and also not easy. This is a story about love and faith and family and pain and the shedding of one way of believing and the brave pressing into an entirely other way.

This is a grown-up, clear-eyed story of faith, told with so much soul and laughter and grit and elegance and plainspoken truth that it leaps off the page, straight into your heart. What a gift.

Shauna Niequist

INTRODUCTION

Dear Friend:

    This is meant to be the introduction to my book. But the idea of introducing this intimate and unexpected book in the way that authors are supposed to do such things seemed too far away and formal to me.

    Yet I knew I couldn't drop you straight into the story, like someone pushing you off the pier into the lake before you were ready to jump. I respect your jump too much to shove you right in. I was stumped for a long time about how to welcome you to these pages, but one day in North Carolina, it all became clear.

    My friend Rachel and I organized a conference called Evolving Faith, and—miracle of miracles—people showed up. We spent two days with you or people like you—the readers, the thinkers, the dreamers, the question askers, the wilderness wanderers, the status quo upenders, the ones who wrestle with God until they walk with a limp. The first year was a powerful, spirit-filled, wild, imperfect weekend. On the final night of that particular weekend, I stayed until I had spoken to every single person who wanted to talk to me. I stayed until the entire retreat center emptied out and I was left there alone. I walked up the stairs to the empty stage, still carrying your stories, your notes, your letters, your faces with me, and looked out at the quiet pews for a few minutes before going back to the hotel. It is one of the great honors of my life to carry your stories with me. You tell me about your marriages, your children, your friends, your churches, your work, your traumas, your dreams, your hopes, your sorrows, how your stories intersect with my work or my books. I carry so many of you with me every single day.

I went back to the hotel after that night to eat rather terrible takeout pizza and drink Costco wine with the good folks we had invited to speak. My friends Austin, Mike, and Jeff curled up on the floor with me. Rachel popped in to say an early good night and good-bye to us all because she was still nursing her youngest child and needed to sleep. We waved her off to bed and promised that next year she would be right there on the floor with us. I had on my jammies, and it felt so good to finally rest. We had poured out everything we had for two days. So we chatted and laughed until we cried the way you do when you're exhausted.

Then Jeff asked me how long I had stayed at the retreat center, and I told him what I told you: I stayed until it was empty. He asked me how I, an admitted introvert with chronic pain issues, had managed to talk to so many people so personally for so long. I paused before answering because I suppose I could have said all sorts of things about the importance of connecting with readers and the duty of care a conference organizer carries to those who show up; if I really wanted to be mercenary I could talk about brands and sales and good responses on experience surveys.

But the honest first thought that sprang into my mind when

Jeff asked that question was this: *Because I love them.* So that's what I told him. "Because I love them."

And it's true. I often feel as though we are alongside of one another. You're never faceless, nameless entities to me—you're my friends, the ones who read my words. I think about Jen and Precious, about Nichole, about Shauna, about Jonathan, Laura Jean, Idelette and Tina and Musu and Nish and a million other names and faces. You're real to me, not simply "readers," but somehow, over the years, we've become friends. Even if this is our first introduction, I have carried the idea of you and your stories as I wrote these words. (Also, hi, nice to meet you.)

That moment of answer was when I knew I couldn't pen a typical introduction to the book you now hold before you. I needed to introduce this book from a place of love and connection because it has been written from a place of love and connection. We carry one another's stories. If you have read my other books or heard me preach or listened to me on a podcast or whatever, you've carried some of my story. And in turn, I've carried so many of your stories for so long. Your e-mails, letters, messages, conversations are here with me somehow still.

And it's time I trusted you with this particular story of mine.

This is a very different book than I've ever given to you. It's much more personal. (It's also much weirder—don't say I didn't warn you.) I promise you—I kept trying to write a different book. I kept trying to write the book that I thought you wanted or even the book that I wanted to write instead or the book the almighty "market" deems bestseller-worthy (spoiler: it usually involves 5 Steps to Hustling Until Your Dreams Come True without Any Real Work, but that isn't my usual jam).

But instead, *this* book persisted. This is the work that needed to be born. I have no earthly idea why that is, why some books simply demand to be born, come into our lives with such insistence until we've served them well and released them out into the fresh air. So after fighting with this book—after trying and failing to write a whole other book instead—this is the story that demanded to be told first. And so here she is. (Maybe now she will give me some peace.)

In these pages, I finally tell you the whole story of my devastating car accident from a few years ago. This car accident changed my body and so changed my life. But I also need to tell you about the time that I went to Rome and met the Pope (it's complicated). It's about my father's legacy, about messy miracles, about the experience of healing in all its frustrating forms, about the ways that God speaks to us and meets with us and surprises us. The journey of this book begins on a road here in British Columbia, but that road leads to Rome. And then the road leads right back out of Rome for me. I'm going to take you by the hand and lead you through the last few years of my life, pointing out the ways that I found God hiding in plain sight in my ordinary life, never where I expected.

Meister Eckhart, the fourteenth-century German mystic, once said, "God becomes and God unbecomes." I don't think I fully understand this but these words are a soul-knowledge to me, deeper than simply intellectual understanding. That unbecoming became an unlearning to me over these years. The more I tried to keep God contained, the more God insisted on escaping from my fetters. Every time I built a box for God, God transcended that box . . . while still somehow often abiding within it to meet me there. Every time I think I have it figured out—*this is how God acts, this is who God is, this is what God will do, this is what God expects*—that reorienting, bracing, dangerous Love becomes and unbecomes again. And so I have been made and remade and unmade over and over again in response to the Ancient One. We place a lot of emphasis in our culture on "right learning," but there is something to be said for the value of "right unlearning" and "right relearning." We have to be committed to unlearning the unhelpful, broken, unredemptive, false, or incomplete God if we want to have space to relearn the goodness, the wholeness, the joy of a loving God.

Telling this story has been, to me, a wild balancing act. Every time I began to tip in one direction, God would counterbalance me with the rest of the story. This is because every story we tell of our lives has a counternarrative—we know this. We hope to tell the truth as we understand it in this moment.

The metaphor for my unbecoming and rebecoming, for the ways that I have had to learn and unlearn and relearn God the past few years has been at the altar of my physical body. The fulcrum in the middle of this book, the axis upon which the story turns, is in Rome. There may be times when you find this story too much or too little—I want you to stay with me until the end anyway. My hope is that any time I lose you, you will trust me enough to stay with me until the end because we have walked many roads together, you and me.

I should probably warn you right up front that I love Jesus with my whole heart. I have zero chill on this topic. I think he's worth following, and that can get me into trouble. I have never evolved past Jesus: I still abide in the shadow of his wing. Oh, and I'm pretty into the Holy Spirit. I am one of those messy mystics, insisting that God is actively and intimately leading us and speaking to us still, delighting in disrupting me. I can't apologize for these things, but this is me warning you so that you're prepared when it gets weird.

Dear friend: I feel as if I couldn't say with conviction that I love you if I didn't tell you this story. If I hid or downplayed or minimized what God has become and unbecome in my life. Truly I couldn't continue on in any sort of public life or ministry without this book being written. The truths I have learned in these years have changed me on a cellular level. Everything that I am today was formed by what you will read in these pages. It has felt as if my soul has been hiding in the Holy of Holies for a bit too long now, and I'm ready to fling wide the heavy draperies and throw open the windows, welcoming fresh air into the space between us. I want to invite you into this. My story, at last.

I think you're here because you are tired of our systematic theology books, our rules and our boxes for God. You don't feel like you fit in the narrative that because you follow Jesus or are a good person your life turns out perfect. You're tired of hearing that God is a judge and a rule book and a small, narrow white room, a formula, a predictable map.

No, you're ready to stand on the cliffs and feel the wind in your hair, to encounter the wilder Spirit, to have your rules of God broken by God him—or her—self. I think you're here because you are ready to remember that Love can be a comfort and a warm cup of tea, absolutely, but God can also take your breath away and leave you whooping with tongues of fire.

That's why I'm here anyway. And there is a seat next to me—it's all yours for these pages. May the Spirit move as she will move, and may we move with God toward Love.

Love,
S.

PART I

❧

Spirituality is always eventually
about what you do with your pain.
—Fr. Richard Rohr

CHAPTER 1

LUCKY

*W*hen I woke up in my minivan, the first thing to register was the smell of Tim Hortons coffee. At the moment of the crash, my coffee had exploded out of the cup holder, hitting the windshield and the roof, raining dark roast everywhere.

A panicked face appeared at my car door. He was frantically banging on the door, and a horn—my horn—was blaring. I lifted my head up off the exploded steering wheel airbag slowly, disoriented. Automatically I reached over and unlocked my door, which he swung wide open. I groaned at the small movement. I could move my arm, though—that was a good sign.

"You okay?" he shouted over the horn blaring. "Are you okay? Ma'am? Miss? Can you hear me? Are you okay?"

I had no idea how to answer that question. Was I okay? I had no idea.

My whole body began to shake. I couldn't seem to move on purpose. Everything hurt right up close to me, everywhere, especially on my left side, but my brain was still far away, wondering indignantly why I smelled coffee and smoke, why the horn wouldn't stop screaming.

"Don't move," he said. "Don't move at all." I could hear sirens in the distance. Another car was crumpled on the side of the road; I was horizontal across the highway, facing the west even though I had been driving north. The sun was still somehow shining. I could smell hot tires, see black tire skid marks everywhere. Who knew that crashed metal had such a horrible smell? The airbags were still burning against my body; there was grit in my teeth.

"I saw the whole thing," the man at my window shouted. "I saw it all. Good God, you're a lucky girl. Holy hell. I saw that whole thing. Don't move now; just wait for the guys. The guys are coming. Those are my guys—I'm a volunteer firefighter, miss. Hang in there, now. Jesus."

"Bri, could you wipe the tears out of my ears?" I was lying flat on my back, strapped to a metal board, encased in a neck brace in the hallway of our emergency room triage. It was an out-of-the-ordinary night at our regional hospital. Maybe there was a full moon; I don't really know—after all, I wasn't near a window, and I wouldn't see the sky for many hours still. All of the rooms were full, the beds were scarce, the doctors were scurrying, the nurses were triage efficient, reinforcements were being called, and I was entirely focused on enduring.

I wasn't actively crying. I was just weeping quietly without intention. The tears kept coming, pooling in my ears, leaving me feeling like I was swimming underwater. I waited until I could barely hear the noise of the hospital before I asked Brian to wipe my ears out.

"Why didn't you say something sooner?" he asked, sweeping a hospital-grade tissue into each of my ears.

"I didn't want to be a bother," I said. "I'm sorry."

"I think that ship has sailed," he said. "This whole mess is super inconvenient for me—bad timing, Styles. Could've planned this better, eh?"

He has always called me by my maiden name when he's feeling tender. He placed his hand gently on my forehead and moved my hair back from my face, tucking it behind the collar of the neck brace, holding my gaze.

"Honestly, woman," he gently scolded, shaking his head slightly. "Where else would I be?"

A while later, he said, "You're still shaking, Sar. Are you cold? I heard they have heated blankets down by the nurses' station. I'll be right back with one. The nurse told me where to go."

"Not cold, no," I chattered. "Just still can't stop shaking. I'm sorry."

"I hate the smell of hospitals," I whispered when he returned with the heavy, warm blanket. "I've had enough of hospitals this year. I don't want to do this anymore. I just want to go home."

"You sound like your dad," he said. "We just finally got him home, and now here you are. We'll get through this—you'll see."

"I'm just so tired. I want to go home."

We fell silent. Eventually a woman sat down near us, wrapped in crude bandages up her arms. "Wow, what are you in for?" my husband asked her sympathetically.

For twenty years now, I've watched my husband make friends everywhere he goes. Once we were in the checkout line at a Walmart Supercenter in Texas when I realized we had forgotten the milk. He said hello to the cashier and began unloading the groceries while I turned to run back to the dairy case. By the time I returned with a jug of milk in my hands, the cashier was wiping her eyes with a tissue and he was nodding sympathetically as she said, "And, of course, that just brought up all the feelings of when my dad left us. . . ."

Brian turned to me and said, "Babe, this is Susan; she was just telling me about her Thanksgiving."

Of course she was. I wasn't even surprised by then. People trust him almost immediately. It was part of why I fell in love with him: he was so earnestly and unapologetically interested in people; he liked almost everyone, and they loved him for his unfussy genuine interest, his warmth and steadiness.

Me? I rejoiced when the grocery stores installed self-checkout lanes so I wouldn't have to ask the Susans about Thanksgiving. My husband thinks self-checkout lanes are an abomination, taking jobs from decent working people: another symptom of disconnection in our society. There is an old adage that married people start to look like each other as the years go by: this is certainly true in my capacity to make small talk with strangers. I have grown from a girl who just wanted to get her milk without making eye contact to someone who is on a first-name basis with the checkout ladies at my corner store.

I often joke that he was born the best kind of grown-up: capable and kind, never in doubt to what is The Right Thing to Do, the kind who makes you relax because someone *good* is in charge. He's the sort of man who started saving for university when our babies were all still in diapers, who knows how to fix drywall and plant gardens, who renews insurance and files taxes early by himself, who sticks with the credit union out of principle, who coaches middle school basketball because he genuinely loves to be there. And so, of course, he is here with me.

Back at the hospital, it turned out the lady across the hall from us had been on the wrong end of a pressure cooker explosion earlier. "That'll teach me to cook a meal," she said with a good-natured chortle. "Carryout meals from the White Spot from now on, that's what I told my husband! How about you two?"

"Car accident," he replied. "My wife was in a crash. We're just waiting for the CT scan to open up. Busy night here."

"Poor girl," she said sympathetically. "Drivers these days. I hope it goes well for you both."

I couldn't turn my head to look at her, but she sounded kind.

"I'm sure I'll be fine," I said to the ceiling.

"Of course you will be," she said. "You were lucky."

They kept chatting as the clock above my head ticked steadily. I felt relief that they had found each other in the hallway, because I could be silent and awake yet distracted by their conversation. Each time the minute hand moved, it sprang forward with a click and wavered from its new position in time. It was the only thing other than ceiling tiles that I could see from my strict vantage point.

It seemed impossible that just hours before I was out for a drive. I had been enjoying the peace of the moment when alongside the back highway, in the fields at the base of the mountains, I had caught a glimpse of a heron, swooping across a low pond in a field. It had felt like a good omen for the day.

I often see a heron at key moments in my life. It began one day when I went for a walk at the lake in our town. It was late spring but a pleasant cold, the kind that wakes you up a bit after a winter of too much coziness and too many candles. I stuffed my hands into my mittens and tucked the gray hair at my temples behind my ears. I hadn't gotten my hair colored in a while and it showed, I hadn't slept well and it showed, I hadn't felt like myself in a while and it showed. I was tired and so I needed to walk in the fresh air to wake up; I was looking for something like a deep breath.

The sun was already low in the sky, and the trees were asleep with early spring cold. I stood on the edge of our little community lake and watched the geese beginning to swoop in after winter, the clouds resting like a gauze scarf on the mountains rising dark in the deep light.

I turned toward the reeds and there, standing still, staring right at me, was a blue heron, slender and regal, neck relaxed, her long legs in the water among the reeds. I've always loved blue herons: their blue-gray wings are like twilight, their elegance rooted in their ubiquitous domesticity. I remember hearing once long ago that herons were considered a good omen: when the First Nations indigenous to my homeland would head out on a fishing expedition, the sighting of the heron meant it would be a worthwhile hunt because the bird embodied patience and wisdom, both necessary for survival. They can be seen as protectors and guardians, sentinels. A friend once told me that this is because a heron is equally at home in the water, upon the land, and in the air—she goes with the flow and works with the elements around her rather than against them.

I stood silently, watching the great blue-gray bird caught between mud and cold water and a darkening sky. Herons are a regular sort of bird, ordinary and unspectacular and yet beautiful.

Someone just up the path exclaimed and pointed to the sky: an eagle. There is a nest way up high above the pines at the other end of the lake. Eagles are spectacular when you see them out in the wild, stern and beautiful and awesome in the truest sense of the word. Their stark white helmets, their golden beaks, their black feathers swooping through the sky are arresting. Their wing strength is economic and thunderous. Around me I could hear other people gasp as the predator dipped lower over us before gliding higher and then disappearing into a horizon I couldn't imagine. She lived so far above the rest of us. Everyone looked up, yearning for a glimpse of her again.

It took me time to learn to love the heron's lesson. Perhaps that is because my father has always been an eagle sort of man. My life's rock, he was grounded and assured in his way of seeing God. His certainty was safety for me as a girl: he prayed with such confidence and spoke with steady conviction about God and life. And my father loved eagles, loved the image of the eagle, loved the references to eagles in the Bible.

Whenever any of us became ill or grew weary, my father would speak and pray the words of Psalm 103, a constant source of prayer and promises to him, over us—not as a magical incantation but almost to remind or reorient all of us toward what he saw as the promise of a good God for us . . . "who redeems your life from the pit and crowns you with love and compassion, who satisfies your desires with good things so that your youth is renewed like the eagle's."*

My parents became Christians in their thirties, welcomed and baptized into a subcommunity of Christianity descended from the Pentecostals and charismatic renewal movements in cultural expression and mode of worship. Our origin movement is sometimes called the prosperity gospel, but in my experience it was more accurate to call our branch the Word of Faith movement. There were prosperity gospel influences, of course, but the excesses weren't as strong or obvious back then—not to me anyway. No, the emphasis was on the Bible and on our particular interpretation of it. There was always a strong emphasis on supernatural provision and healing for our bodies, our minds, our finances, our relationships, all of the pain points of being human. The reason why we emphasized it is because we were the ones who were often broke and sick and miserable; the ones attracted to prosperity gospel are there for a reason, and it's rarely greed. In my experience, it's desperate need. And we found goodness there. We learned God was good and so all of the things that steal, kill, and destroy life are not of God, not ever. We believed in the power of our words, we revered the Bible, we were convinced that faith was a muscle we could work to consistent results. There are gifts of such a way of understanding God, but there are shadow sides to this as well.†

The image of eagles has seemed like my father's faith to me. The way he spoke of their soaring as metaphors for renewal

---

* Psalm 103:4–5, NIV.
† I write about this much more in my second book, *Out of Sorts: Making Peace with an Evolving Faith* (New York: Howard Books, 2015).

and strength, for overcoming, was always part of our encounters with suffering and sickness and pain. On that day, the eagle reminded me of my father: its solitary strength and dignity, its certainty in flight. I've heard that the eagle is "the master of skies" in some cultures because it is believed to be the creature with the closest relationship to Creator, moving easily between the physical world and the spiritual world.

I've wanted to be more like my dad almost every day of my life, but I am still me: unable to be too certain because of my uncanny ability to see eight sides to every issue and my yearning for peace above all else, unable to be much more than on the outside edge of the inside, with an eye on the ones for whom the truth is perhaps not true.

My father would turn toward the prophet Isaiah's words at moments of faltering or failure or exhaustion: "He [God] gives strength to the weary and increases the power of the weak. Even youths grow tired and weary, and young men stumble and fall; but those who hope in the Lord will renew their strength. They will soar on wings like eagles; they will run and not grow weary, they will walk and not be faint."*

Many years ago, I walked away from the Word of Faith movement. I deconstructed my own faith, and I am still in that middle place of figuring out how to rebuild something that will be worth dwelling in for the years ahead, something worth giving to my children as a legacy of faith.

On that day, my gaze returned to the blue heron still standing patiently in the mud and water, and something in me looked

* Isaiah 40:29–31, NIV.

between the eagle and the heron and then said to the bird in the water, *All right, then. I see.*

Perhaps my father encountered God in the promises and strengths of soaring eagles. While I still believe, deep in the core of my being, in the goodness and abundance of God, I also believe God is as present in the darkness as in the light, in the valley as in the mountaintops, in my suffering as in my victory. As I watched the heron, she swept her wide wings open and lifted up from the reeds, taking to the sky, the tips of her wings touching the water as she rose, creating ripples.

Standing on the ground between a heron and an eagle, I suddenly knew where I belonged: in the mud among the reeds in the water *as well as in the sky*. I can see God most clearly in the particularities of mundane unnoticed miracles now—small children dancing, the way my son prays, my girls piled in our striped hammock with their neighborhood friends, one wide table filled with food for the lonely, the proclamation of good news, kids in school uniforms in the dust of a deforested Haiti, sponsor families waiting with winter coats at the airport for Syrian refugee families staggering out of civil war into a Canadian cold, rejected or marginalized Christians singing about the wideness in God's mercy, holding the hand of a beloved friend till her last breath, and one more candle burning on a lampstand to light up a whole room. It is angels on a hillside with common shepherds and kings in stables and virgins having babies. It's uneducated Galileans as ambassadors for God and the eunuch asking, "What is to stop me from being baptized?" and Mary Magdalene hearing Jesus speak her name in the garden.

I need—then and now—the God who sits in the mud and in the cold wind, in the laundry pile and in the city park, who is as present in homework and nightly baths and homemade meals and hospital rooms and standing by caskets. I need a God with teeth and hunger, who embodies grief and joy; wisdom and patience; renewal with simplicity and a good, deep breath; and who even now shows up in the unlikeliest and homeliest of lives too, as a sacrament and a blessing for the ordinary incarnation of feet on the ground and baptism of the water and wings wide in the sky. I have come to love the mud and the reeds, the water and the quiet day, just as much as the feel of the wind in my hair as I take flight and soar.

I was driving about ten under the posted speed limit, traveling at seventy km/hr. It was a nice day for a drive—the highway was wide and practically empty, the day was dry and bright, the mountains standing guard around me, and I was in no hurry. I was listening to CBC Radio 2's classical program, sipping my double-double,* living my best life. There was a sedan parked on the side of the road up ahead just past the small bridge over the creek. As I crossed over, that car hit the gas and swung out in front of me, attempting a U-turn to go back the other way. The driver, assuming that the highway was as empty in that moment as it had been all day, didn't bother to shoulder check to see if anyone was there behind him before swerving into oncoming traffic for his U-turn.

* For the non-Canadians: a double-double is a large coffee with two creams and two sugars, usually from our national coffee chain Tim Hortons.

But I was there, hurtling toward him.

He swung almost parallel across the highway, just as I came up on him. I slammed on my brakes, pulling hard to the left to try to avoid the crash. I couldn't.

I have heard from other people who have been in traumatic car crashes that time can feel like it slows down in that moment, like your senses are heightened and you notice everything, see everything, hear everything—your mind kicks into another plane of awareness for what is happening in that moment and even for what has come before. I can't say that it happened that way for me—I had no life-flashing-before-my-eyes slideshow kick into gear with operatic overtones.

No, I stomped my right foot on the brake with all of my might, swinging the minivan left and away to avoid the impact. I slammed my left foot into the floorboard, using my foot to brace for impact. I remember sucking air into my lungs, like I was about to jump into a cold lake, pulling as much breath in as I could and then holding it.

There was this sickening awareness of inevitability; I remember that. I couldn't stop this, and I knew it already. I knew that we would crash, and the instant sweep of drowning powerlessness hit me long before our vehicles collided. This was no close call I could avoid; this was happening no matter what I did next. The inescapability of this, the impossibility of any other outcome, gave rise to the only conscious thought that I can remember of that moment even now: *So this is how I die.*

And then we crashed.

The next things I remember are the smell of coffee, the horn blaring, smoke billowing, and one man shouting at my window.

❧ ❧ ❧

A different nurse checked on us every thirty minutes through-out the night. The woman with the burns had been moved to another area a while ago. It was just me and Brian again.

"I have never seen the hospital like this ever," said one nurse. "You picked the worst night for this, luv. We are crazy in here. You should have picked a nice Tuesday morning. Saturdays are no good for crashes."

One nurse brought a bolster pillow for my knees and lifted up my legs to place them gently on the pillow. "This will help with the back pain from the brace," she said. "I know it feels like it's making everything worse, but we have to keep your spine straight. Hang in there. This will help a bit. Now, when was the last time we gave you morphine? Are you crying because of pain or because you can't stop crying?"

"Both?" I said. "I can't stop. I'm trying, I promise."

"Good girl," she said, gently touching my shoulder. "It's the shock wearing off. Keep warm, stay awake, let's get more mor-phine going."

"I miss the kids," I whispered to Brian. He told me that my parents were at our house and everyone was already in bed, sound asleep. I wanted to be in their bedrooms, standing over their beds, watching them breathe under their blankets in the quiet of our home. I wanted to tuck them in, pick up their socks from the floor.

The lady reappeared with fresh bandages from her hands to her biceps.

"I'm all set and heading home," she said cheerfully. "I just came by to say good luck to you both before I go. Have a good night." We waved her off with good wishes.

"What was the name of the guy who was at my window?" I asked Brian. "I can't remember his name. It was Doug or Gary."

"Oh, that narrows it down." He grinned. "Only every other white guy in Canada over the age of forty is named Doug or Gary. The only thing that would make this easier would be if his buddy's name was Gord. No problem."

I tried to make my face smile but failed. "He was a volunteer firefighter," I said. "We could probably find him. I need to thank him. He was so nice to me. He saw everything, he said. He saw the whole thing and he knew just what to do."

"We'll find him," he said gently, no longer teasing to try to make me smile. "Don't worry, we'll find him. Right now let's just worry about getting you fixed up."

"He said I'm lucky," I said to the ceiling. "He's seen similar accidents, and he said I'm really lucky."

"I guess that's relative," Brian said.

After a few initial tests and conversations, along with many painkillers, I was resting with my eyes closed still strapped to my board and encased in a neck brace when another nurse's face appeared in my peripheral vision. She peered down at me and said, "Well, you look a hot mess. What happened to you, dearie?"

"Car accident," I croaked—I hadn't used my voice in a while. I felt Brian sit up from his sprawl in the plastic chair beside me. He had been dozing.

"How fast were you going?" she asked while she opened my eyelids wider and examined me quickly. My eyes filled with tears again; they wouldn't be stopped.

"Seventy," I said. "I was on the highway. In my minivan."

"Whose fault was it?"

"The other guy. He pulled a U-turn on a highway without checking to see if someone was behind him. I was there."

"What a jerk," she said without sentimentality. "Well, let's get this show on the road, eh?"

She called for the porter, and he soon appeared to wheel me to an unending parade of X-rays and CT scans.

"Helluva night here," he said to Brian as I rolled beneath the ceiling tiles. We moved through the now nearly empty hallways briskly, Brian holding my right hand gently as he walked beside the stretcher. "What happened to the other guy?" he asked.

"He seemed okay at the scene. His teenage daughter was with him. They were both shook up but walking around. He kept apologizing, but the police charged him with the accident, I heard. I don't know if he went to the hospital."

"Buddy's lucky," he said, shaking his head.

After a full CT scan and examination, we found ourselves in a curtained cubicle with the coveted doctor. "Let's run through what I have here and make sure everything was covered," she said. "In addition to the head injury and concussion, we have the spinal injury through the thoracic spine, the neck—looks like bad whiplash—your left wrist, the left hip, left knee, your left foot, seems to be soft tissue damage with all this bruising everywhere, plus these nasty seat belt lacerations on your neck. Right?"

"Right," Brian said. "That sounds like everything."

"You have a long road ahead of you, but you'll walk it," she said. "You're lucky."

"Yes, so I hear," I said.

"I'll refer you out everywhere for the healing process, but your family doctor will be your hub for the physio, the neurologist, the soft tissue damage, all of it. There will likely be other injuries that surface over time, so prepare yourself for a long road. The concussion will heal with time and rest—ice, stay awake, no screens, that sort of thing. Now, we're a little worried about this—see here on the scan?" She pointed to a dark circle in the image of my brain.

"This spot on the scan? It looks like there is bleeding on the brain. That's the big worry—it could spread or do something, but given everything I think we'll watch it but not panic yet. We'll be sending you to a neurologist tomorrow and doing a follow-up scan. You can either sleep here in the cubicle or you can go home. It's been an insane night here, and we're at capacity for beds, so your call."

"I want to go home," I said. "I just want to go home. I want my house and my kids and my life."

"Home it is, then," she said. She turned to Brian: "You need to watch out for her tonight. If she throws up, if she seems foggy, if her face sags, if her speech starts slurring, if you have any reason to think she's not doing good, you call an ambulance. Got it?"

He looked at me and his eyes softened.

"Got it," he said. "Let's get you home, Styles." He lifted me into a wheelchair and began to wheel me toward his car.

CHAPTER 2

DANGEROUS WOMEN

*T*he morning of the crash, I had been preaching at a women's retreat in the mountains. It wasn't a typical lady retreat, though—for one thing, there wasn't any Wi-Fi and nary a craft table.

We were about two hours outside of Vancouver in the shadow of Mount Cheam nestled into the tall trees, surrounded by countless waterfalls cascading down the rock face. We were one hundred women, all gathered to learn how to rise up together. We were chasing after the idea of sisterhood, of what it means to be women of liberation at this moment in time.

The lead organizer was my friend Idelette, who is originally from South Africa. We've known each other for ten years now, and in so many ways, we have been rising to our full capacity alongside each other throughout those years. She is one of many dangerous women in my life—those are the women who make me braver, stronger, wiser, engaged, and awake, the women who are a thorn in the side of the enemy. They are the ones who challenge me and comfort me. The best friends I've ever had are the women who are equal parts hair-petting and ass-kicking.

Idelette and our friend Kelly coined the phrase "dangerous women" for the women who are a danger to the status quo, who are dangerous to the powers and principalities of this time.

Idelette and I couldn't be more different—down to the fact that I wear comfy sweaters and soft moccasins while she's usually decked out at the school track meet in black leather and stiletto heels. Our origin stories couldn't be more different either, but some part of my soul recognized hers at our first meeting, and she's not been able to get rid of me since—I would probably walk on coals if Idelette asked me to do so.

She had conceived of this gathering as an antidote to the typical women's retreats—she wanted to create a space for the women who feel like they don't quite fit into the Good Christian Lady story, the women who make other women clutch their pearls, the women who feel like zebras in a pasture filled with horses. She wanted the zebras to gather to rise up together.* So we all showed up here, all the way from Winnipeg, Vancouver, and even the United States.

According to the schedule I was handed for the day, we were to open with Idelette's welcome that morning. She stood up in silence before us, her Mohawk swept up, her big earrings swinging. I've been to more than my fair share of women's retreats given my line of work, so I was pretty certain she was pausing before prayer to open the day. We collectively bowed our heads obediently and waited. Instead, she suddenly bellowed the word, "FREEDOM!" like a warrior right into the silence of women. Her cry sent shivers down my spine and I sat up straight. She

---

* A fun fact for you: Did you know that a group of zebras is called a *dazzle*? For real. That just made my day. "A dazzle of zebras" sums up the women in this room.

turned to our friend Melaney of the Musqueam Nation, who began to drum. Melaney sang a welcoming prayer from Chief Dan George and welcomed us to the unceded ancestral land. I don't speak her language myself, but we all swayed like church mothers to the drum that had once been outlawed here.

We were seated at tables instead of in rows. I preached one of the opening sessions on that Saturday in February. I've come to terms by now with the fact that I am a preacher: some people are teachers, some are pastors, some are gentle encouragers. Me, I hit the stage at a run, and I pace and holler and gesture and declare Big Things. Once Brian and I did a tag-team sermon about marriage at church—by the end of the sermon it was pretty clear how opposite our callings are. He sat on a stool with his thick Bible open before him, patiently explaining and teaching through the Scriptures while I proclaimed and waved my arms and jumped in with big statements. He went line by line, and I soared thirty thousand feet up above to talk about love! justice! equality! If I knew how to sing, I'd have burst into "Can You Feel the Love Tonight" by Elton John there at the end.

I believe with my whole heart that the number one place where women should be flourishing is in the body of Christ. So I preached about what it might look like when ordinary women like us rise up in faith, at our full strength, instead of silencing or numbing or dumbing down or retreating in response to cultural pressure. It's dangerous. Women who are awake are dangerous to the powers and principalities around us. We need to stop waiting for permission that has already been given. We've been commissioned to embody the Gospel in every corner of our lives.

I preached in particular from the story of Mary Magdalene's encounter with Jesus at the tomb after his crucifixion. I've always loved this story, but it's taken on new meaning for me over the past little while because in it, I see the embodied ridiculous goodness of God toward women. On this particular day, the disciples of Jesus are in mourning: their Master is dead. Mary goes to the tomb even before sunrise—perhaps to anoint his body with perfumes, perhaps just to be near his body. But when she arrives at the tomb, the stone has been rolled way. She immediately runs to Simon Peter and John to tell them that someone has taken Jesus out of the tomb. The men run to the tomb and look inside. John even walks right into the tomb to verify her extraordinary claim. Sure enough, Mary was telling the truth: it's empty. And so they go back to the place where they were staying (this part of the story always makes me chuckle and roll my eyes—thanks for your help, gentlemen, now we know it's real because the men verified it, much appreciated).

But Mary stays, weeping loudly. She looks in the tomb again, and sees two angels sitting there: they ask her why she's weeping. "They took my Master," she says, "and I don't know where they put him." Then she turns away and sees a man that she thinks must be the gardener. This man also asks her why she is crying. She repeats her sorrow to this man too, begging him to tell her if he knows anything about what has happened to her Jesus.

And that's when he says her name. "Mary."

Every time I reach this part of the story, I feel like I could put my head down on the table—I just need a minute, you know? There is something about this moment that grips me: in her deepest grief, he speaks only one gentle word . . . her name. And it is when Jesus speaks her name that she lifts her head and recognizes him at last. She cries out "Teacher!" in glad recognition and disbelief and joy.

The next thing Jesus says here is "Don't cling to me." A lot of very wise and educated people have written profound and beautiful things about the theological implications of that statement: big thoughts on resurrection and the nature of ascension and incarnation. I'm sure it's all true and right; they are much more educated than me after all. But honestly? Part of me just believes he said that because she launched herself at him. That she ran at him, and clung to him with all of her sorrow and trauma and grief and relief and joy and amazement in her arms. As a mother, I know how kids can sometimes hug so hard that it almost feels like a strangle. I read his statement with the protesting laugh of love—*You're hugging too hard! Let me catch my breath!* Regardless, Jesus tells her to go and tell his brothers. She dances off, the miracle singing in her mouth, proclaiming the good news, the first preacher of the resurrection—"I saw the Master!"—and she tells the other disciples everything he said to her.*

The Church used to refer to Mary Magdalene as "the Apostle to the Apostles." I've always loved that phrase. Despite the cultural liability of it, it was a woman who first proclaimed and preached the resurrection. Because it would have been so much tidier for the early Church if the first witnesses to Jesus' resurrection had been the powerful and well-respected Jewish men, preferably religious leaders, perhaps a whole quorum of them. But instead, Jesus spoke her name at the empty tomb. In a time when women were

* This story as I've related it here appears in John 20:1–18.

not considered acceptable legal witnesses in any court proceeding, here at the resurrection women were the first witnesses and the first preachers. This feels like holy subversion to me.

I love to read this story to roomfuls of women because I want them to see it too—I want them to see that Jesus commissions women to proclaim the resurrection. I couldn't have known as I preached about the importance of women proclaiming resurrection that morning that I was about to descend into my own valley of shadow.

After I prayed over the gathering and sat down, woman after woman would rise up to share her story and then the room would respond with tenderness and power. At one point, we began to sing this simple song together:

> She's got the whole world in her hands,
> She's got the whole world in her hands,
> She's got the whole wide world in her hands,
> She's got the whole world in her hands.

I know that using female pronouns for God can be electrifying for some people, but over the years, that practice has become an important part of my own spiritual formation. I came to the practice late, even after my first book, *Jesus Feminist*, was released, which always strikes me as either laughable or tragic, I'm not sure.

The imagery of God as also female, as mother in particular, has held invitation and healing with just a dash of danger for me. One of my favorite verses when I was a nursing mother myself was from the Psalms: ". . . I have calmed and quieted myself, I am like a weaned child with its mother, like a weaned child I am content."* The imagery of that took up residence in my soul—picturing the way that my own babies became so incredibly full and content and sleepy with my milk, blissed out in security and warm tummies—when I would meditate or pray.

It hadn't always been so for me. I have been pregnant eight times and we have four children. My eldest daughter was my fourth pregnancy, yet another miscarriage occurred between her and my son. There were many days when I thought that the sleep of my own babies would be something I would only witness in kingdom come. A loss—whether early in the pregnancy or not, I have experienced both—is a particularly isolating kind of sorrow. It's almost invisible to everyone else but you, and the loss feels as if it is also all your own to bear.

I began to make the shift in good earnest when I noticed in the Genesis story, as God creates humankind, they said to one another, "Let us make human beings in our image, make them reflecting our image."† Both male and female, God created them, both of them in God's image. Our language's pronouns might be incomplete for such a wonder. I don't use exclusively female or nonbinary pronouns now; I still love the imagery of the maleness of God perhaps because I have good men in my life who embody the hopes of manhood. It's just that now I have room for the femaleness of God too, and that has been healing. Because we all bear the image of God.

So when that song rose up among us, I felt my soul exhale. There is such a different feel in the feminine pronouns for God,

* Psalm 131:2, NIV.
† Genesis 1:26 (MSG).

a different sense of love and constancy from the traditional male pronouns for me. I don't think I ever could have imagined how often in the days to come I would have to return to this moment, to this feeling that God has the whole world in her hands. We sang the roof off the place, and everything felt possible.

There was a quick break in the schedule when I decided to sneak out for a minute. I've grown into a fairly outgoing introvert—truthfully there are few people I can't enjoy for a time, and I now love friendly chitchat at the grocery store. But that hasn't changed my default setting of needing a bit of quiet in order to recharge and to feel human again.

So I ducked out to the minivan and pulled out of the retreat center. I knew that there was a Tim Hortons just a bit farther up the highway, where I could grab a coffee and then listen to the radio for a bit. I planned on being gone for thirty minutes— drive out for fifteen minutes, drive back for fifteen, listen to quiet no-voices music, no one would miss me, and I would be restored.

That was the plan, anyway.

I didn't return to the weekend, of course.

I texted Idelette from the ambulance to tell her what had happened. I heard later that she set out a lit candle, right onstage, with my name tag on the table as she told the gathering about the accident, and then the women there all prayed for me together. They kept that candle lit throughout the entire weekend as I went to the hospital and eventually came home at about the same time that they were all headed to their own homes. I had prayed over them that morning, and then they carried me in prayer. The reciprocity of sisterhood is something that sustained me even in that moment, I think: the mutuality, the way that we carry one another's burdens and pray for one another, back and forth and back and forth. I've grown wary of spiritual leaders who like to do all the praying for others but never remember that they also are in need of grace and healing and a community of women around them.

At the end of the weekend, Melaney and another friend named Kallie from Treaty 4 territory out in Saskatchewan wrapped up each of the women in the room in a beautiful red, black, and white printed scarf.* Together with Idelette, they commissioned the women like Mary was commissioned at the tomb of Christ on Easter morning, to go and tell what they had seen, what they had heard, what they had experienced through the Holy Spirit. At that moment, the sun broke through the clouds and lit up their faces like an omen while I lay on a stretcher, breathing the oxygen of their dangerous prayers.

A few weeks after the gathering of women in the mountains where I had crashed, Idelette and I met alongside the Fraser River for a catch-up over lattes. At the end of our visit, she pulled out a beautiful red-and-black Coast Salish wool blanket on behalf of our friend Melaney. She stood up in the café as an emissary and wrapped the blanket around my shoulders, the weight of it a mantle, and spoke Melaney's written words over me like an ancient blessing.

She spoke of the sacred history of blankets in her tradition, how they were used in ceremonies as regalia, as currency, as

* This scarf was designed by Heiltsuk artist Ben Houstie.

gifts to honored guests, as spiritual coverings, as a rite of passage for a new name or a marriage or a new home or a life-changing event, as anointing of leadership, as covering and protection for those who speak for the people or who share wisdom and spiritual teachings.* Then she rested her hands on my shoulders and offered prayers for courage as, like Mary, we also became a voice of resurrection. I nearly lay down on the floor of the café, overwhelmed, like I was at an old-fashioned healing meeting and the Holy Spirit had just fallen down on me.

As I drove home, the blanket still around my shoulders, I took the back way alongside of that ancient river. I unrolled the windows, letting the wet, damp cold of our spring sweep into my hair until everything, even my pain, smelled like the water and the land.

---

* My deepest thanks to Melaney Gleeson-Lyall for this moment.

CHAPTER 3

THE FIRST MIRACLE

*L*et me back up a bit. Because I should mention that my father was sick.

Just a year before the accident, his heart began to falter, a slow progression of heart disease. It was genetic—he portrayed none of the common indicators, and so the possibility of early intervention passed him by. By the time we knew he was sick, he had lost so much weight his clothes hung like bedsheets on his already small frame; his normally ruddy former-redhead's complexion became the color of cement. He appeared to be dying before our eyes, his heart shutting down in fits, starts, and attacks.

A year before, he had chased my children around the playground, scampering effortlessly up the slide and swinging from the monkey bars and picking them up in his strong arms. Of all the people in my life to become sick, my father was the last that I would expect. He stopped drinking alcohol twenty-five years ago. He's never smoked. He exercises, he eats so well it cramps my style, his energy is such that he runs laps around us all. But apparently the hereditary nature of heart disease doesn't much care if you order the salad three times a week.

That year, before we knew what was happening to his heart, we went out to a restaurant to celebrate my mother's sixtieth birthday. It was a loud and chaotic dinner as only a group of fifteen people including six little children can manage to produce. We feasted and we laughed and we toasted my mother's life. He was sick, but we didn't know how sick yet.

Soon after that feast, we were all horribly ill with food poisoning. The only two spared were our then one-year-old baby, who'd had her own baby food to consume, and our five-year-old, who simply refused to partake of Greek food because it had "specks" in it, much to my irritation at the dinner. It seems she had the last laugh (and now she has justification for her pickiness about the sprinkling of parsley and oregano for the rest of her life).

In the early morning hours of that following Sunday, my father had a heart attack likely triggered by the food poisoning's strain on his heart. He was stabilized at the hospital, and finally the answers began to come in as the seriousness of his situation became clear at last: massive blockages in all of his arteries, some operating at less than 10 percent of their capacity. His heart wasn't working anymore, and it could give up at any moment.

We began to negotiate our new normal. My mother stripped her life down to him alone, unable to leave him for any amount of time because of the inconceivably real risk that he would drop dead at a moment's notice. We watched him grow old before our eyes. In just those few months, his hair turned snow white, he became thin and impossibly thinner again.

One day when he had a presurgery exploratory procedure, as I stood in the hospital hallway with my mother, she seemed suddenly fragile to me. In moments of crisis, I transform into an irritatingly competent Mrs. Rachel Lynde,* all bustling and capable, cheerful and tender. We watched the operating room doors, waiting for his reappearance as elderly people were rolled out with regularity. When they rolled my dad out of those doors, I didn't recognize him. My eyes slid right past him; it was just another old man on another stretcher. My mother moved toward the old man, and I was confused: Why was she going to this stranger?

It took a minute for my brain to realize that this was not just any old man: this was *my* old man.

We experienced that familiar shift that happens as your parents become sick or grow older. We needed to be strong for them. We needed to take care of both of them in these days. Brian cut the lawn. My sister's husband, Adam, managed work needs. Amanda called my mother every single day. We hosted the big family dinners at our homes instead of at their home, and my mother tried to hide how much she missed being the one to cook and present the turkey.

We prayed for a supernatural healing almost every single day. We believed it was possible because we had seen it with our own eyes before this. We used to joke that it was too late to tell us healing isn't real anymore—we had all already experienced some form of healing from the major to the minor: fevers going down, anxiety departing, one leg that grew to match the other's length. Part of the reason why my parents converted to Christianity years before was precisely *because* of an experience with supernatural healing. My father had suffered with ulcers and anxiety

---

* This is not the last reference I'll be making to L. M. Montgomery's fictional characters; brace yourselves.

his entire life; it was his torment and affliction. When his young wife began to steer the family toward church, he was reluctant. He was distrustful of religion and authority; he truly disliked anyone telling him what to do. This combined with his natural skepticism did not make him an ideal candidate for conversion.

But one night more than thirty years ago, he sat in our house in Regina and dared God to heal him. He had heard the preacher say God healed, and he had asked that man if he meant it. The minister, bless him, said that yes, it was real, and yes, he believed God could and would heal. That night, God called his bluff, healing my dad not only of ulcers but also of anxiety. A man of his word, he became a man of the Word and never looked back. We had no need for a family theology of his suffering. God was his great healer then; wouldn't that be true now too?

And yet, now, everything failed and he was still sick unto death. No matter what we believed for him, he wasted away.

The night before his major heart surgery arrived, since our little city hospital doesn't have a cardiac unit, I drove the hour to the hospital where the procedure would take place, in New Westminster just outside of Vancouver, to be with my parents and my sister in these hours. Who knew what the next day would bring to us?

We sat in the sparse shared hospital room. We knew both the risks of the surgery itself in the morning and the risks to him particularly, we knew the recovery plan, we had read all the pamphlets, and we had made the mistake of Googling the incision images. My sister was morbidly curious about what his scars would look like, as if she could stop being afraid if she knew what would come afterward.

Our family has yet to meet any tension that we won't seek

to release with a bad joke. We have our own shorthand of totally inappropriate humor, deployed in moments of stress and exhaustion and anxiety. We are primed for these sorts of stressful days with many references to movies we are embarrassed to admit we watched together—and then we laugh over Austin Powers quotes until we finally cry.

We've always said that my father's love language is to be teased: nothing makes him happier than when his daughters or his sons-in-law give him a hard time or make a joke at his expense. So we teased him mercilessly that night, making jokes about his drab brown hospital pajamas really being prison jammies and how the law had finally caught up to him. We made fun of his roommate's never-ending chitchat about the price of gas despite my father's deep dislike of small talk. We quoted *Seinfeld* episodes. We were brave and filled with fake laughs and light banter, and my heart was breaking.

God was running out of time to heal him the way my father thought he should be healed. I worried about his unanswered prayers as much as I worried about his broken heart. I worried that he was going to lose his God even if he kept his life, because the God he knew was disappearing like steam on a mirror with every resolute step toward this surgery.

Tomorrow they would break his sternum and spread wide his ribs and cut into his heart. They would pull veins up and away from his legs and move them to his chest; he might die, he might not recover, he might not wake up, he might be completely fine. No matter how much we grinned and tap-danced through the evening, the specter of his mortality sat beside us on the hospital bed, patiently waiting to be acknowledged.

We did not acknowledge the fear we felt, the grief of his freckled chest—one we all knew as intimately as our own bodies—being broken open. We did not acknowledge the possibilities. We were tirelessly positive until my face ached from smiling, and I expected Churchill to tell us to stand down from carrying on so calmly. We said good-bye cheerfully, like we were expecting a picnic the next day. We had no idea how to behave, how to be, in this unfamiliar story.

And so I cried as I drove the minivan over the bridge spanning the Fraser River. I kept imagining him laying in that hospital bed alone that night, with that roommate who wouldn't stop talking about the quality of the yogurt cup on the lunch tray as he watched the clock tick toward his seven a.m. surgery time. I wondered if tonight—with words I already couldn't remember—was the last time I would hear his voice.

For more than twenty years I have kept a now nearly transparent, often folded e-mail on cheap computer lab paper torn off a dot matrix printer tucked into my Bible. When I went to university, I moved from Calgary, Alberta, to Tulsa, Oklahoma, in a time when that meant something different than perhaps it does to us today—back then there was no social media, there were no smartphones, and international landline calls were expensive and rare.

I was eighteen, far from home, on my own. The university assigned me my first e-mail address, and my very first e-mail was from my father, written up on his arrival back home in Calgary from dropping me off at school. In that e-mail, he shared

Scripture with me, told me he was proud of me, released me from being homesick, encouraged me to create a good and beautiful new life there, to put down roots, to be happy apart from my family.

Reading his words on the old Windows 286 computer wasn't enough, so I printed them off on the communal printer, folded them up, and tucked them into my Bible. I pulled them out to read when I was homesick or sad. And those words set me up for that first semester, which set me for that year, and I don't think it's an overstatement to say that university was the first time in a long time that I felt like myself. Like most young adults, I shook off any dust that didn't belong on me and moved forward to the life waiting for me. Sometimes we need the good-bye in order to even imagine moving ahead.

When I arrived home from the hospital, our children were already sound asleep, and Brian was up waiting for me. We held each other in the kitchen for a while, silently. When he went to bed, I stood in the living room in the darkness, lit only by street-lights, waiting.

Eventually I sat down at my laptop and wrote my dad an e-mail, hoping that he would check his contraband mobile phone before the next morning's surgery. I wrote everything I needed to say to him, not shrinking from the good-bye that needed to be said just in case. I wanted him to go into that operating room knowing how well he was loved and how grateful I was for him.

By dawn, I was up and back on the highway, driving back

over that bridge over the Fraser River again to the hospital just to see him one last time with my own eyes.

My father's last words before they rolled him into the room were to my mother: *I love you*. He took off his wedding ring and handed it to her. He hardly ever takes it off; it's as familiar to me as my own wedding ring. He met her eyes and pressed the white gold into her palm. Her fingers closed around it. Forty-two years of marriage passed between them. She stepped back and unfastened the thin gold chain of her necklace, threading it through his ring, letting it drop heavy against her heart.

I stood beside my mother and my sister as he went on without us. After all of the flurry of activity to get to this moment, my mother's stillness and the room's quiet felt strange. Her hands went to his wedding ring, hanging heavy around her neck as we began the long wait.

Eventually he will come out of surgery and they will tell us that he will live.

He will suffer horribly in the weeks of recovery. When we are first invited to see him in the cardiac ICU, my sister will faint at the sight of him and my mother will need to leave the room to cry as hard as she needs to. I will sit beside him alone while he recovers in the ICU, knitting while the machines breathe for him and he twitches and sometimes kicks against the pain, moaning thickly over his breathing tubes. The anguish he feels even in his anesthetic sleep squeezes the room. He is in pain, and it takes too long to figure out how to manage that pain.

For weeks, he will swear that he would never do it again—

he would rather die. Every time someone at the hospital lightly refers to his scars as "the zipper club," it will take everything in him to not cheerfully throw something at their head. It will take six months before he admits that this ordeal was worth it.

Together we will speak of the promises of eagles while he is grounded in one hospital bed after another. For men like my father—men used to caring for others, priding themselves on being the provider and the rock—the gentle ministrations of his family are almost too much to bear; he can hardly bring himself to receive my sister's care after his surgery, my arm to lean on while he walks in his hospital gown down the hall at the pace of the sick, my husband's insistence on shoveling the driveway for him. His anger at his body for this betrayal will be palpable, sometimes directed at us, but somehow we will know that he isn't angry at us for this, he is angry at his body and perhaps even angry at God. I will pray his favorite prayers of renewal and strength over him and mean every single word with my whole heart: I will believe for him what I cannot believe for myself anymore.

We will become reacquainted with the mercy of weakness, the blessedness of receiving, the slow walk toward wholeness that doesn't skip over the suffering. His brutal experience of healing—cracking open his ribs to the light so his heart could be mended, the surgeries, therapies, and months of mending—will take root, but there will be a sadness to even this. None of it will go the way he thought it would go. He thought that his healing would look more like the soaring of eagles into renewal: instead, he will scrabble and fight, march and suffer toward wholeness.

He will keep healing, slowly, but he will not be the same as he was before—we all see that. Oh, his body recovers. He'll feel better than he did for the year before the surgery. But something in his core will be different. His heart was broken, and the mending nearly killed him. His body will return to strength, his color will return, his energy will return, but something about God has been reset along with his bones.

And he will have his own questions over this suffering. He will wonder where God is in the pain. He will think that if it weren't for love that filled him and surrounded him and sustained him, he wouldn't have bothered. He will learn what it is to hear your own heart beat and know that it's a miracle. He will learn what it means to love God and to endure unanswered prayers and unexpected grace for suffering. He will begin to understand the miracle of healing is wider and more expansive than it was thirty years before, when he dared God to heal him one prairie night. He will learn what it means to pray on the other side of a strange and painful ordinary miracle.

A few months later, he will tell me that he printed off the e-mail I wrote to him that night, telling him good-bye, just as I had printed off his e-mail all those years before. He will tell me that he often read those words of a daughter's farewell while he was healing to remind himself why he was fighting for each heartbeat in his ravaged chest. He will tell me that he's started to go for a little jog at lunch and it feels good to be outside again.

We will all learn that this is also love: the stern and steady presence of abiding with what cannot be changed, of the kind of love that shows up to work, and of finding this life just a bit more precious because of a possible good-bye and an imperfect, slow renewing. We will learn that these are also our miracles: bloody, corporeal, painful miracles.

My father was brave enough to reimagine healing. We had an inadequate theology for his broken heart and my wounded body and our twin sadness.

His line of sight to God changed and, rather than assume God had disappeared, he shifted his position, and the real miracle is that God came back into sight again. In response to the change of his spiritual landscape, my father became a student, not an expert, and he practiced remaking himself in response to his new vision of God.

He had, as always, gone before me to make a path. As I struggled and suffered and faltered after my own near-death experience, I wondered if I could be as brave as he was, if I could be as faithful, if I could make eye contact with my unanswered prayers and keep praying anyway.

CHAPTER 4

THE BLESSING
OF ROCK BOTTOM

*I*t's never a good time for a car accident. But honestly, I would have organized this differently if I were in charge.*

I was already a bit weary before my minivan spun across the highway, if I'm being honest. As I told you, my father had been sick the previous year. A close family member was diagnosed with cancer, and we learned my husband also carried the genetic markings and had passed them to our children. And the year before all that: Maggie.

Maggie was a surprise to our family; we had three babies in four years and those kids were now engaged in the work of growing up. I used to refer to our kids as the tinies, but I can't do that in good conscience anymore. As of this writing, my eldest is taller than me by four inches and still growing, and the rest of them aren't far behind. That year, they were finally all in school, the long-awaited sweet spot for most parents. I felt good about

---

* Narrator voice: She was not and never would be "in charge."

49

our new season of life as I began to work more as a writer and preacher. After all of our miscarriages, I felt ridiculously fortunate to have three children.

And then, right at the time in my life when my doctor pronounced me to be a woman of "advanced maternal age,"* Maggie came into being, unexpected but so welcome. Brian wondered aloud if she was my "desire-of-the-heart baby"—perhaps some part of me knew that pragmatically we were done, but my heart was still longing for one last little baby to make a fool of myself over. He knew me too well—I was over the moon about the possibility of Maggie even as I tried to catch up with the reorienting of her imminent arrival. It was bewildering and complicated and beautiful, all at the same time.

When I first became a mother, I was in my late twenties. And the experience of becoming a mother changed me inside and out. I know it doesn't happen that way for everyone, and I'm not saying my way is prescriptive or normative, but there it is: this has been one true, clear altar where I meet with God and I am transformed. I not only uncovered something true about my own self, but I connected with God in a whole new way; my ideas of God and life were hung out on the line in the bright sunshine of this new revelation.

That's not to say that birth itself was easy or even textbook for me. After all, our son, Joseph, was born in the parking garage of our apartment building because we weren't able to make it to the hospital in time.† We used to joke that we decided to pursue

---

* Thanks, Doc!

† I tell more of this story in my first book, *Jesus Feminist: An Invitation to Revisit the Bible's View of Women* (New York: Howard Books, 2013).

a home birth for our third, Evelynn, because after the experience of Joe's arrival in parking spot seventy-four, my husband swore off trying to put me into cars while I was in labor—he had never recovered from that day. So by contrast, Evelynn was born in water at our home, where I was attended by the kindest and most capable of midwives. I still look back at Evelynn's birth as one of the shining stars of my entire life—the whole experience from start to finish was so grace-filled, so healing, so peaceful. *What a way to end my experiences with childbirth*, I thought. It was perfect.

The rhythm of being pregnant and giving birth, while never easy, became the great metaphor for how I encountered God. The more I experienced pregnancy and birth in all its mess and glory, loss and life, the more I uncovered the devout parallels between how women experience birth and how the Holy Spirit often "gives birth" in our souls. Mothering was where I found God, and even now it is where God continues to somehow find me too.

When I spoke or wrote about birth, I always talked about how as soon as I had delivered a baby, I would break into joyous laughter. My husband would always cry, and I would always laugh, tipping my head back with relief and joy and clutching that new life to my breasts.

And then we found ourselves unexpectedly expecting this one last little baby.

And everything was just *different*. I was different; the pregnancy was different. I felt disoriented, like I was having to reorganize the story my life was telling. I thought we were going in one direction as a family, and now we were regrouping. The big kids were all thrilled and so was I, but I couldn't help but feel that things were not as they had been.

I was exhausted for most of the pregnancy. Three other kids will do that to a woman, I know, but Brian also had a job change that meant he was working longer and more stressful hours. And having a baby in your late thirties is quite a different experience from having a baby in your twenties, I assure you. My next book was due right before the baby was expected, so instead of resting during the pregnancy, I madly wrestled words onto the page and submitted my second book in between all of my travels for ministry. I told everyone who would listen *how incredibly happy we were*, and then I would go to my shower every night like clockwork at six thirty p.m. to cry with disorientation and exhaustion for fifteen minutes straight before emerging with a smile on again, so incredibly fine.

And as her birth loomed nearer, I knew how it felt to go into birth feeling fully empowered and ready, strong and capable, but this time I felt exhausted and depleted. The baby was clearly much bigger, I was older, life had been too full. I remember saying to Brian that I was rethinking having a home birth again. I thought rather wistfully of a clean hospital with a capable anesthesiologist. But I quickly snapped myself back: this is not how I give birth! I don't medicalize birth! I am a natural birth advocate! I will give birth the way that I always do! It will be beautiful, dammit!

Instead, on the day that I went into labor, I quickly realized that my instincts had been right*—I did not have it in me to do this well. I had made the wrong call. All three of my other babies had a very similar progression for a quick and straightforward labor. This baby was completely different. Just a few

---

* Pro tip: Always pay attention to your instincts the first time. It saves a lot of trouble.

hours into labor, we transferred to the hospital because when my water broke, there were indicators that the baby would need a pediatrician on hand. In the ambulance, I agreed to any and all drugs that they would give me, and by the time we got to the hospital, I had lost the thread of myself. The rest of the baby's delivery was a blur to me, a blur of pain and powerlessness.

I can now remember thrashing on the bed, fighting off the midwives and doctors, transcendent with pain, unrecognizable to myself. I kept begging for someone to help me, over and over again: this was too much and I couldn't do it. The baby was in distress and I was gone in every way, unable to do the work that needed to be done to save her, but it was too late for anything else.

The turning point happened when Brian caught me in his arms and looked me right in my frenzied, hot eyes and said, very slowly and deliberately, "Sarah, no one is coming to help you."

I fell silent, staring at him in confusion. No help? There is always help. *I want help.*

"There is no more help," he said looking right into my eyes so I could see that he meant it. "You are going to help yourself. No one is coming to save you or the baby now, Sar. You will save both of you. You are the only one who can help—no one else."

In a weird way, those words, "No one is coming to save you," calmed me down. I hung on to him and did the work; I was going to save both of us now. She was born silently in four very intense pushes to a very stressed room of doctors. The pediatric team immediately snatched her up and began interventions. She had to be intubated because she had swallowed meconium and wasn't breathing. After what felt like an entire revolution around the sun, as empires rose and fell, she sputtered and began to wail.

They announced her at ten pounds, seven ounces, and brought her to me at last. I howled like we had just survived a war. She was my desire-of-the-heart baby, my miracle baby, and it had been a battle to bring her through the valley of death to her first breath of life. There was no laughter on my lips this time: I shook with sobs, covering her vernix-coated and blood-slick head with my tears. Brian held us both, and I just kept saying to her, like a survivor who can't believe it, "We made it, we made it, we made it."

Afterward, we were cleaned up and left in peace to heal and nurse. Physically I was exhausted and spent. But emotionally I was reeling from the last hour or two of my labor in particular, struggling to figure out what it meant or if it meant anything at all, feeling like a failure and a warrior at the same time. The truth is that birth is never not a miracle—I know that. It's never not the best and the worst at the same time. I kept returning to the sight of Brian's face and his words that no one was going to help me, that I had to save us both, and then I would remember that I'd done it. Whatever else happened, we were saved.

We named her Margaret Love—Margaret means "pearl" or "bringer of light and gift of God." She was a gift from God right from the start, and now I know that she is my pearl of great price too. I remember reading in an old favorite book* that pearls are for tears—which are assumed to be sad, but some of

---

* *Anne of the Island* by L. M. Montgomery, natch.

our happiest moments can involve our tears. My tears when I finally had her safely in my arms tell me something so true and deep about our tears and the way we are baptized in them too, even in the grief and the pain blending with the most powerful love and strength. Later, I learned that the pearl is also a symbol for Mary Magdalene's tears, her tears of gratitude and recognition at the empty tomb. And, of course, we named her Love because she was created in love, by love, for love, and we believe love wins, always and forever.

I wrote out the whole experience—because this is what we writers do to figure out what we think about things—and sent it to my dearest friends as one part testimony and one part confession. I needed witnesses for this moment in my life, I needed them to know how I had crashed so completely, lost myself so thoroughly, and survived anyway, saved us both anyway. My friend Glennon wrote back to me, "This is the blessing of all your plans falling apart, all your control being lost, even your very image of yourself being erased: your person carries you anyway. This is the blessing of rock bottom. I pity folks who have never lost their minds. How do they know they're not in charge, and that that's okay?"*

After Maggie's birth, I pushed through and completed all of the edits for that second book, and it was published. I did most of my media tour from my living room, with her nursing. (There are so many podcasts from around the release of *Out of Sorts*

---

* If you haven't yet read Glennon Doyle's books, please go to the library or the bookshop and get all of them.

with the smacking and squeaking sounds of baby Mags in the background.)

Now, after this accident, I was determined: I was going to save myself again. I would persevere. I would recover. I would not miss a single commitment to preach. I would not miss my book deadline. After all, I am someone who succeeds. I am not easily sidelined.

I went in for another CT scan of my head: the blood clot had broken up and I was in the clear. See? Miracles. I crossed my arms defiantly.

I told everyone who asked: Look at how lucky I had been to emerge from this whole experience relatively fine. (I was already crafting my own tidy story.)

It would be fine. I was fine. I was already *so incredibly fine*.

But it turns out that you can't hurt your skeleton without hurting your muscles, and you can't hurt your spine without hurting your nerves. You can't receive a concussion without consequences. You can't be in a car accident without bearing the marks of it. My days were spent resting, going to doctors' appointments for X-rays and consultations, standing on one leg for the physiotherapist and promising to do my stretches, lying facedown on a massage therapist's table, taking drugs to help with pain, investing in heating pads and ice packs, wondering what the gigantic swelling in my left foot was and then dismissing it as soft tissue damage.

There isn't a single part of us that lives in isolation from the rest of what makes us human. Our bodies aren't simply along for the ride of our souls. And as the weeks went by and the full nature of my injuries emerged, I kept enacting the grand deception that I was completely fine.

I wrote almost every day, hour after hour, struggling to land a book that had begun to feel out of control. I wrote and wrote and wrote, thinking somehow that more words would help create a book. I never missed a contracted speaking engagement. I cooked suppers and signed permission slips and cleaned the house and clipped little fingernails.

I also had constant migraines. The trauma to my neck, my spine, my back, my hips was lingering and intensifying. I had many days where I could barely walk because of either my back or my hips or my foot. I was submerged in grief and pain and doctor's appointments and anxiety. My thinking was muddled. I was in chronic torment. I couldn't walk.

And still I would not quit writing. I thought rather wistfully of simply stopping. Of putting my hand up to admit that I was circling the drain and everything hurt and I just needed to catch my breath. But then I would carry on just as I had done before Maggie's birth: This isn't what I do! I finish commitments! I write books! I am a professional! I am capable! I can get knocked down, but I am a woman who rises! *It will be beautiful, dammit!*

The first panic attack of my life happened on the highway at night. I was driving to a friend's house and it was dark, of course—the days are short at that time of the year, and the sun sets by four in the afternoon. I was on Highway 1, headed west, when a car in the merge lane on my right decided to race into the spot ahead of me instead of the spot behind me. The driver sped up on my right-hand side, the same side that the other car had swung out at me, and leaped into traffic, barely missing my van as the merge lane ended.

I slammed on my brakes far harder than the situation warranted—I was never in any real danger—and skidded to the side of the road, pulling out of traffic and nearly into the ditch. Unthinking, I turned on my hazard lights, laid my head on the steering wheel, and burst into tears, clawing at my throat because the air would not flow in and out of my lungs. The fear filled my nostrils and my lungs and my ears like a rushing, and I coughed and slobbered. After some time, my breathing returned to normal but my body kept shaking. I felt dissociated from my body, as if I were above myself or outside of myself, watching my hands tremble and my arms wrap around my body in an attempt to stop the shaking, my feet bouncing, my teeth chattering, my jaw aching, my shoulders up to my ears. I was being choked by the sensation that the crash was happening all over again—the feeling of impact, the sensation of inevitability. I kept breathing, counting my breaths, until I could put my hands on the steering wheel again and eventually drive home.

The next day, I turned in my third book to my publisher. It was more than twice the size it was meant to be. I turned it in with relief and tried to celebrate the way I always did at this milestone of pressing send on a manuscript. I couldn't muster up the celebration for simply surviving. I made spaghetti for the family that night. When I lifted the pot to pour the sauce over the noodles, my left hand gave out as it had become wont to do and the entire pot and the spaghetti and the dishes we have had since our wedding crashed to the floor. I stood in the center of the shards of dishes with noodles and sauce dripping down the counters. Then I turned to the sink for a dishcloth—the mess wouldn't clean itself; I might as well begin to clean while I was crying.

It was right about then I received an invitation to meet the Pope.

PART II

❦

Believing takes practice.
—Madeleine L'Engle

CHAPTER 5

WALKING IN ROME

*W*e stood shoulder to shoulder in the center of a crowd of people in the small room. There was barely space to turn, but we were rotating in tight circles just the same, our heads tipped back to look up, up, up to the ceiling. Our mouths were open and a quiet hum of awe filled the room. We were standing in the middle of the Sistine Chapel at twilight. Candles and low lamps lit the room.

Above us, Michelangelo's famous frescoes filled the sky. The chapel was centuries old, pilgrims were mingled with the tourists, many were weeping. Perhaps they were overwhelmed with the beauty. Perhaps they were overcome with fear at the possibility of a Judgment Day like the one depicted by Michelangelo on the wall behind the altar. Perhaps being in this particular room was the culmination of a lifetime of saving and dreaming and longing. Perhaps they were feeling the weight of history, the presence of the stories. Perhaps the Holy Spirit moved them. I stood in the chapel and wept right along with them.

I was leaning almost entirely into the arms of my husband, who was half carrying, half supporting me through the Musei

Vaticani as the sun set over Rome. Even though I looked like one of the overwhelmed faithful, the reason for my tears was far more corporeal—I was in excruciating pain.

It had been four months since the accident, and rather than getting better, I was steadily growing worse. My left foot was swollen, and I could barely walk on it without weeping, but X-rays revealed nothing. My spine remained out of alignment, resulting in radiating pain through my upper back. My left hand had become useless, unable to button up the coats of my children. The spaghetti dishes were not the last casualty to my diminished strength and mobility. The stabbing pain in my hip often caused me to stop in my tracks and yelp aloud as I fumbled for whatever wall or person was near enough to keep me from crumpling. My thinking became foggy; I was forgetful and vague. The low-grade pain was nearly constant, but then every few days, I experienced what I began to euphemistically refer to as "body days" when pain shone out from more than a dozen spots in my body like a constellation, relegating me to the couch until the light had dimmed.

The light was blazing hot in my body while we stood in the chapel, Brian holding me upright as I wept without ceasing.

One day, just a couple months after the accident, a very official-looking letter attached within an e-mail arrived from the Vatican.

We are happy to invite you to join Francis, Bishop of Rome, to celebrate the Holy Spirit in the Golden Jubilee of the Catho-

lic Charismatic Renewal. The event will be held in Rome this June. We look forward to enjoying your presence in this Pentecost prophetic ecumenical celebration, and have reserved a special place for you at the Vigil with the Bishop of Rome.

You can imagine my wonder.

I am not nor have I ever been Catholic. In fact, in the churches of my childhood we were frequently anti-Catholic, referring to former Catholics as having been "saved *out of* the Catholic Church" much like the lady who used to be a Wiccan had been "saved *out of* witchcraft." Like most wrong thinking, this was corrected by proximity to those whom I had been taught to distrust. Thanks to my friends who were cradle Catholics and those who converted to Catholicism in their adulthood, I had learned about their vibrant and devoted and varied expressions from South America to Rome to my own neighborhood.

But beyond an occasional viewing of *Sister Act*, an appreciation for their sense of mystery, a still-gnawing distrust for the institution, and an appreciation for Jesuits like Thomas Merton and Franciscans like Richard Rohr, my familiarity with the tradition was minimal. I'm near the lowest rung of the Low Church* ladder compared to the High Church grandeur of Rome.

---

* I use the term "Low Church" to differentiate my tradition from other more liturgical traditions. Originally a pejorative term, "Low Church" was meant to distinguish those Protestant churches who de-emphasized ritual and liturgy, sacraments and authority. The Catholic Church would be considered "High Church." Even though the distinction was meant to be insulting at the beginning, I've grown to love the phrase "Low Church" because I like the vision of Church and faith that is down in the dirt.

Where in the world had this invitation come from?

At the end of the letter, they told me to check in with a certain Bishop Q for more information. All right, now here was a name I knew. Back when Brian and I lived in Tulsa, the church we attended was led by a man we affectionately called Pastor Ed. Almost twenty years later, we reconnected through mutual friends when he invited me to preach at a gathering he had convened for people just like us—charismatics who were embracing a more ecumenical expression, rooted in a re-embrace of ancient practices of the Church. Reconnecting with Pastor Ed was a great joy—even though I nearly fell over in a faint when I saw him in a white collar and learned that he was now called "Bishop Ed" because he had converted to the Episcopalian tradition and was now leading a monastic order. It was through Ed that I met Bishop Q at that ecumenically diverse gathering for liturgically minded charismatics.* (Say that three times fast.)

We all shared roots in the Word of Faith movement and we had all departed from that theological interpretation of Scripture. However, while I remained staunchly in the charismatic

---

* I've used the word "charismatic" multiple times so far, but perhaps I should define it as I use it. The Greek word *charisma* means "gift." The early Church used that word for the gifts of the Holy Spirit, for instance as listed in 1 Corinthians 12:8–10 as well as other places in the New Testament. A charismatic Christian is one who believes that those gifts are still in operation today and often practices them. However, a charismatic isn't a denomination or a sect of Christianity; rather, there are charismatics in almost every single denomination of Christianity. There are charismatic Catholics and charismatic Baptists and charismatic nondenominational folks like myself. The charismatic movement has roots all the way back to Pentecost, but the modern movement as we understand it was reignited at Azusa Street in the early 1900s and then again in the 1960s, which resulted in the birth of several new Protestant denominations and movements as well as the Charismatic Catholic Renewal movement.

tradition enhanced by my personal embrace of the ancient practices and sacraments, Bishop Q had also converted to the Episcopalian tradition, eventually becoming a bishop himself, all
while holding on to his passion for us Low Church charismatics. It turned out that he also had deep friendships with fellow
charismatic Catholics connected to Rome.

I hadn't spoken to either bishop for a few months, but I immediately e-mailed Bishop Q and asked him, in a very saintly and
holy sort of manner, because I am super mature, "Um, WHAT?
Did I just get invited to Rome . . . to meet the Pope?* Is this your
version of a joke?"

Bishop Q assured me that, yes, I had been invited at his
request to celebrate the fiftieth anniversary of the Catholic Charismatic Renewal movement along with Ed and several other
friends from that same gathering. Apparently Pope Francis
wanted to celebrate their momentous anniversary with a grand
demonstration of ecumenical unity. He had specifically asked
that people like me—Protestant charismatics with deep roots
in Pentecostalism from all around the world—be present at
the Golden Jubilee's prayer vigil in solidarity with their Catholic expression. Bishop Q thought I was just what Pope Francis
had in mind for this weekend's prayer for unity in the universal
Church, and he wanted me there with them.

Well, then.

I called my mother to tell her about the invitation. Obviously the invitation was an honor. And just as obviously, I
would not attend. Attending hadn't even entered my head yet.

---

* I mean, they do know I wrote *Jesus Feminist*, right?

I had never been to Italy, had never left my children for that long of a time. Besides, who goes to Rome? Not me or anyone I know.

And I will be honest with you, my friend: I held serious critiques toward Catholicism. For instance, for all the beauty around their theology of the Eucharist, it is a closed table, which means the bread and wine is only available to Catholics in good standing. I wouldn't be allowed to receive communion with these folks. And if there is one thing I'll go down swinging for, it's that the bread and wine is for *everyone*. If there isn't room at the table for everyone, then we need a new table. As my pal Jonathan* often says, "If we're controlling the guest list, then it's not the Lord's table."

My views differed from the Catholic Church's on everything from women in ministry to LGBTQ+ inclusion to the notion of even *having* a Pope, let alone their unresolved legacy of trauma from the residential school system here in Canada and the ongoing waves of revelations of their institutional cover-ups related to child abuse. This would not be a quick and uncomplicated yes for me.

So I told my mum about the invitation and she was silent for exactly three seconds before informing me that I was *absolutely going* to Rome to meet the Pope. She and my dad would move into our house and run our circus for the entire ten days required for the trip, and that was settled.

Brian and I talked it over for days before eventually agreeing with my mother in the end. We would hold our compli-

* Jonathan Martin said this in his podcast, *Son of a Preacher Man*. The episode is "Open Table."

cated feelings, remain unsure, and show up with open hands and open hearts anyway, carrying the complexity with us.

And then we bought our airline tickets before any of us could change our minds.

Brian's mother, Leona, was less impressed with the invitation. She had been raised a devout Catholic and left the Church before Brian was born. My mother-in-law is the middle child of fifteen kids, their large family attending Mass in their small Nebraska town of three hundred. It's not a stretch to say that the Catholic Church was the most dominant presence within her family, shaping their daily decisions and long-term directions.

Leona always described herself as not truly becoming a Christian until she had an encounter with the charismatic Church in her thirties. She was born again, she said, for the first time: saved *out of* the Catholic Church into a real relationship with Jesus. Her conversion was complete, dramatic, and a total break with the faith of her childhood. In her new-believer zeal, she managed to offend almost everyone in her family at least once. Eventually everyone mellowed as the years passed. Leona recognized her mother's devout faith as equally valid to her own. But she remained suspicious of the Catholic Church, of priests, of rituals, of sacraments, of mystery and authority.

So she was cool toward the notion of us going to Rome— Why would we go there? Why play into the institution's dominance? Why did we feel the need to go to Rome when God was not living in Rome any more than with her in Omaha? Our presence could be seen as tacit approval of the Catholic Church, couldn't it? Those were fair questions, but we had no answer for her except that we genuinely felt we needed to show up for this moment, which she supported.

And let's be honest, it's not every day you get an invitation to travel to one of the most ancient cities in the world and meet the Pope.

Ethan Hawke/Julie Delpy movies notwithstanding, certainly not every twentysomething heads to Europe to ride a night train and drink wine with strangers while having philosophical conversations about the nature of love and life. Brian and I are part of that overwhelming majority. No gap year between or during or after university for us: we were far too serious and purposeful—and poor—for such nonsense. We were grateful for our scholarships and made good on them. We married young and went right to work: we had bills to pay and a shared working-family background suspicion toward incurring debt and anything as frivolous as "happiness." We couldn't fathom a life other than that which our parents had—a good steady job with a good steady paycheck and a reasonable mortgage to pay while living within our means. I know—we were adorable.

On our first date, he took me to a burger joint called Bogey's. He drove the wide streets of Tulsa in his maroon '86 Monte Carlo whose back seat we were later delighted to discover was just roomy enough. The restaurant's decor celebrated Humphrey Bogart's movies, and the Ms. Pac-Man game in the arcade was in prime condition. We ate greasy burgers and fries, laughed with our friends, and then we went to a Tulsa Oilers hockey game with eight other couples. Brian still says that he first began to fall in love with me that night: when I stood up during a fight on the ice and hollered at the players that my granny could fight better than that and loudly booed them with all of my heart. We married in Tulsa and flew to the exotic state of Florida for our honeymoon, even though we weren't really hot-weather beach people.

All that to say: we have never really traveled together. I hardly knew anyone who had gone overseas until I was in university—to me, it was akin to meeting someone who casually mentioned a holiday on the moon. At our current stage of life, we had a houseful of small humanity and my weird job was more feast or famine than we usually liked when it came to our income, so our holidays were usually staycations—we stayed home and Brian worked on fixing up our forty-year-old split-level house while me and the kids went to the lakes nearby. I traveled for work as a preacher, sure, but there is a vast difference between the streets of Paris in the spring and Cleveland's conference centers in the winter.

But now, for the first time, we were going to Italy.

Brian became utterly devoted to the earnest American Rick Steves's travel guides for Italy and Rome. I pinned sights to see and packing tips for my wardrobe on Pinterest. He planned the entire itinerary, including public transit and local inns for us while I created a document for the care and keeping of our four children at home with NATO levels of detail, logging every Girl Guides meeting and school hot lunch day, field trip and science project for the ten days ahead, along with Care Cards in case of emergency and phone numbers for poison control. I bought a new black dress from Reitmans along with black pantyhose to meet the Pope—I had not worn pantyhose since 1999, but I figured meeting the Pope was a sufficiently formal occasion to warrant new pantyhose. My mother threatened to cancel if we didn't have an up-to-date notarized will in her possession before getting on the plane, so for the first time in our lives, we wrote a real last will and testament. We packed our bags. We kissed our children good-bye. We hugged my parents. I tucked my pain meds into the bags next to my journal. We drove to the Vancouver airport, and then we boarded the plane bound for Rome via Toronto.

We were on our way.

Once we arrived in Rome, we caught a taxi to our pension. The heat of Rome enveloped us when we walked through the terminal doors, making us languid, and my hair began to curl. Our driver gave us an impromptu tour on our way to the pension, pointing out ancient buildings and interesting sights. The impossibly narrow roads, the choreographed chaos of traffic, the ease with which we moved in and out of traffic as if dancing was almost as riveting as the architecture.

We were dropped off at our new home for our visit, a short walk from Piazza Navona. We got out of the black taxi and I stood on the cobblestones, looking up and around me. It felt as if I had time traveled. Just down the road, I could see the piazza with her grand Fountain of the Four Rivers in the center. I couldn't wait to hobble down to see it. But first Brian carried our two suitcases up four flights of stairs while I was loaded into the ancient creaking freight elevator for the ascent. We were shown to our room by a friendly woman and eventually found ourselves alone.

Brian walked over to the bank of tall, narrow windows stretching from his knees all the way to the high ceiling. The inside shutters groaned when he folded them open into an accordion before swinging the leaded window wide to the street. He leaned out, then turned, beckoning me over to the light.

"Can you believe this?" he said softly as if afraid of waking us up from the dream. "It's real. This place is real. We woke up in Canada and now we're in Italy."

We gazed down into the street: the scent of jasmine and cigarettes wafted up to us, the noise of conversations in loud Italian from the small café tables along the alleyways rose along with the heat from the sun on the cobblestones, the putter and surge of scooters while the lazy breeze lifted the sheer curtains up around us like a fluttering veil. The heat was lazy and soporific.

We moved toward each other in our long-practiced way, my arms sliding around his waist so my head rested on his chest right at his heart, his arms wrapping around me to hold me close, his chin resting on my hair before he turned his head. We held each other at the open window for a while, breathing in Italy together, our bodies softening and uncoiling. In the street, someone began to play a cello. Soon the player was singing a song we didn't know in a language we couldn't understand. I lifted my face and kissed him until he closed the shutters and the room returned to intimate darkness.

∾ ∾ ∾

We had a few days in Rome before the Jubilee celebrations were set to begin and we would meet up with our companions for the weekend. We were well aware that we may never be back in Rome again, so we decided to make the most of it. We took the mornings to sightsee, but in the afternoons, we returned to the room so that I could recover from my exertions, elevate my foot, straighten my back, rest my hips, take my painkillers, and then reemerge to carry on.

I wore red lipstick every single day, and Brian swore the feast in heaven would be entirely composed of pasta carbonara. In the evenings, we wandered the neighborhoods of the old Jewish ghetto and the piazza surrounding the vast Pantheon. We drank carafes of bright wine in the sunshine and made entire meals of tomatoes and basil and mozzarella. We listened to historical tours via a phone app as we wove through the Colosseum and Palatine Hill and the Forum. We sat back-to-back on stone benches before the Arch of Tiberius, eavesdropping on passing tour groups. We drank espresso and took selfies on the Spanish Steps while limoncello gelato dripped down our fingers. We toasted an unknown bride and groom out with their guests for photos at Trevi Fountain with our espresso, and then we stayed, listening to the water and the music of language until the stars came out.

As the days went on, my body became more weary, my pain more unmanageable. I had barely been getting through the days back home, so I began to lie in bed for longer periods and Brian began to rise early to see the city without me as I lay prone in the darkened room. My spine ached and my hips rebelled when I rose from the bed, my foot screaming in anger with each step I took outside. Brian came back to the room at midmorning with photos of the Tiber River at sunrise and a croissant for me. I tried not to mind.

On our last evening in Rome alone together, we strolled the streets slowly, Brian matching his pace to mine. The next day, we would board a train for one night in Umbria because we wanted to see something of the countryside before coming back to Rome for the weekend's festivities. We wandered into shops, browsing with the lazy aimlessness of tourists who are out of money. The cafés lit the candles on their tables, and the light winked at us in the darkness. We talked about what we had seen and the marvel of it all.

Years ago, before I became more acquainted with the indigenous story in Canada, I used to say that we were a young country. Now I know that simply isn't true—Canada is just as old, just as established as any European or African or Asian nation. We simply erased that history, pretending Canada sprang up with European settlers a few centuries ago when in actuality there were ten thousand years of diverse nations here. This is true, and yet still in my town most of the homes were built in the 1960s and '70s. We don't have many old buildings, not like this, not like Italy. Our town was built around family farms—we have a Costco, but I drive by fields of new lambs in the spring when I go to church. Our cities feel new, even if the memories of the land are ancient.

We don't have cobblestones and ancient buildings perhaps, but what we do have is the created world, still there, still breathing around us like a friend we haven't lost touch with just yet.

We may not have cathedrals and forums, but we have the cathedrals of the pines and the forums of wildflowers, and we have our own myths.

Often when we are out in the woods, Brian will see something—a waterfall perhaps, or a dale filled with ferns lit up with filtered sunlight from the tree canopy above us—and he will say, "You know, where I'm from, that would deserve its own state park," and shake his head in disbelief. He means that for us—he from Nebraska, me from Saskatchewan— back home, this small thing, overlooked by locals, would once have been the whole point of the trip for us.

The sight of Mount Baker from Highway 1 in our hometown makes us look at each other in wonder almost every single week to say, "Can you believe we get to live here?" Even after all these years here, we can't get over the fact that this isn't our holiday; British Columbia is our home. It's easy to take your home for granted, to think that everyone gets to pick blackberries on the side of the road while walking to school, everyone gets to see a heron gliding low over the water while the eagles soar above, everyone gets to take a picture of a black bear lumbering through the neighborhood in September. Everyone gets to rest hot feet in bright cold creeks without names on a summer day, everyone can walk on a phosphorescent carpet of green ferns in the woods, everyone gets to grab a double-double from Tim's and take the long way home.

We take for granted what is familiar to us. It's the way of it. So we wandered through the side streets of Rome in the dark, stumbling upon churches and nooks and statues without names. To everyone in Rome, this isn't a holiday; it's home. They forget that not all of us have Gothic spires next to the convenience store, not all of us know the local unwritten rule that you don't drink cappuccino after nine in the morning, not all of us know what real pasta tastes like, not all of us have evenings like this. We found a lonely, empty ruin run over with cats, illuminated by streetlights, and said, "Back home, this would be the whole point of the visit." But here it was just one more story to walk by, one more sight we almost couldn't see because there was too much to take in.

We wandered along Via della Maddalena into a small piazza with restaurants on the cobblestones. There was a tall church on the piazza too, rising up with white columns and bright yellow walls, the blue door surrounded by ornate stonework as only the Baroque period could produce. When I saw the name of the church, I smiled—it was Santa Maria Maddalena, a church named after Mary Magdalene, the disciple whose story has so captivated me back home. We took a seat at a table under a white umbrella and ordered a bottle of wine from the waiter, who sniffed the cork long and loud before pronouncing it good. Bri lifted my feet up from the ground and tucked them into his lap, his left hand lazily around my ankles so my hip could rest from having to hold me up, the other on the stem of his wineglass. It had taken us three full days to finally stop talking about the logistics of our life—the kids, school, our parents, our sisters, our work, our church, our finances—and to begin to dream again together, to talk about ideas and hopes, to sit in easy silence like this, to blur where he stopped and I began.

A woman with bright platinum hair glowing in the darkness walked to the steps of the church just across from our table as we looked over our menus. She wore a crimson evening gown and seemed to entirely belong in it, the way I belong in leggings and cardigans. A man was with her; he carried a black violin case, but his violin was under his arm. He opened the case and put it at her feet. They stood at the bottom of the steps of the church and, after a few tuning bow strokes from the violinist, the woman began to sing. Her expansive voice rose up in one of Puccini's most famous arias—the only one I could recognize by name, thanks to the one opera CD I purchased in university—"*O mio babbino caro.*"

Time seemed irrelevant to the place and the moment. We sat enraptured and listened to her sing aria after aria into the piazza while people ate and talked over her. Others around us ordered food and paid their bills and fought about the kids while we encountered God. My hands were clasped over my heart. I was unable to look away from her; Brian had his eyes closed, his face tipped up to the sky. When she finished, her voice falling down out of the atmosphere and disappearing into the street again, there was a smattering of applause and people tossed coins into the case while she bowed gracefully. She began to walk away while her violinist gathered his case of coins, tucked his violin under his arm, and followed her, I assume, to the next restaurant. We looked at each other as if we had just surfaced from a dream.

"Back home, this would have been the whole point," I said finally.

"I could go home now," he agreed, "fully satisfied."

We ordered artichokes and poured another glass.

"It's no Bogey's," I said, "but I guess it'll do."

∽ ∽ ∽

The next day, we took the train out of the city up into Umbria for a night to experience Italy outside of the chaos and noise of Rome. We stayed in a small Etruscan town called Orvieto, balanced on a rock cliff overlooking the rolling hills with walls surrounding the perimeter.

After a meal and a siesta, we spent the afternoon within the magnificent Orvieto Cathedral from the fourteenth century known as the Duomo di Orvieto, with its famous black-and-white-striped facade and golden buttresses with an interior of floor-to-ceiling frescoes and altars of relics. We had the place to ourselves.

We stood at the altar, and there I lit a candle: perhaps selfishly, I prayed again for God to heal me. I prayed for some sort of a miracle.

"It doesn't have to look the way I think it should, God," I bargained. "I don't need a shiny, immaculate miracle—I'd settle for a down-in-the-dirt miracle that just takes the edge off."

I looked up into the light straining against the alabaster glass; I missed the sky already. I wasn't meant for this enclosed world.

That night, Brian nearly carried me back to the hotel. I could barely walk anymore.

"What if it's always like this?" I asked him that night in the dark. Our bodies were pressed together in the small bed—the Italians do not make beds for Nebraskans—and yet we were wide awake.

"What if it's always like this?" I repeated. "What if I'm always three steps behind you? What if I'm always in pain? What if I can't clean my house or pick up the kids or just be in the world like I used to be? What if the kids forget what I was like before this? What if it gets worse? What if I can't walk anymore? What if I just keep getting worse, week by week, until my life has disappeared?"

Brian was silent.

"I'm afraid," I said finally. "I'm afraid. It hasn't gotten better; it's only gotten worse. It's getting worse."

He turned over to me and propped his head on his hand, looking down at my face. The tears were leaking out of my eyes, pooling in my ears. He lifted the corner of the white sheet and wiped them away.

"We'll handle whatever comes together—we always do. I don't think this will be our life forever, but if it is, we will do it together."

He lay back down. The rural silence enveloped us. I thought he had fallen asleep. Then he said quietly into the dark, "Don't lose hope, Styles."

The next day, he woke up early again and went out to see the town while I rested most of the morning. There had been a strong American presence in the town during the Second World War, and he wanted to visit their barracks because his grandpa had served overseas in towns like this one. I lay on the bed and posted pictures of our trip on Instagram.

On our way out of town, we stopped at the market and bought him a new wedding ring. He had lost his original wedding ring at a job site years before when he was working as a carpenter after we left full-time vocational ministry. Five euros later, I slid the ring onto his finger, he kissed me against the parapets of medieval lookouts, and we left the hillside fortress for Rome's big event.

CHAPTER 6

THE MISFIT OF ROME

*W*e returned to the noise and oppressive heat of Rome. After an afternoon of rest, we walked through the cobblestone streets to the restaurant where we would meet with the rest of our companions for the remainder of the week. It was a mismatched crew with few exteriors in common—priests and bishops, as well as our Bishop Q and Pastor Ed and a few ragtag evangelicals or evangelical-adjacent folks like ourselves.

As one guest after another arrived and introductions began, I realized that Bishop Q's wife, Annie, was the only other woman at the table. Each guest introduced himself with impressive credentials and educational achievements, titles and affiliations. They were there with their assistants and support staff. They had flown in from the Sudan, from China, from Bolivia, from London. They were repeat visitors to Rome, had weathered a few Popes. I began to feel pressure to make myself sound as impressive as possible, to tout every achievement, play up every role of influence, every accolade, to make sure that these important men knew that I had earned my place at the table. Truthfully I'm rarely easily cowed, but that night in Rome, surrounded by important and influential men in religious collars, wearing their authority so carelessly, I felt thoroughly out of place, for everything from my faith tradition to my education to my sex.

Perhaps I'm contrary by nature, but usually when I feel this kind of pressure to measure up and convince others of my value, I will then stubbornly present myself as unassuming and as unimpressive as possible. I choose to disrupt the contest of importance. I quietly improvised an introduction in my mind: *Hi, I'm Sarah. I am not a Catholic or a former Catholic or interested in converting to Catholicism, but you're all very lovely, I'm sure. I'm from a church tradition that is distrustful of ordination and hierarchy (which is why I love it), and I speak in tongues. I'm a self-taught theologian with zero credentials, and I have a T-shirt that says "Internet Famous" that I wear to irritate my husband because once I started a viral hashtag on Twitter.*

It was our turn for an introduction for real now, and everyone shifted in their seats to look at Brian, waiting for him to introduce us. Instead, he looked at me and smiled. "I'm here as her plus-one," he said easily, leaning back. "My wife is the one you want to know."

The entire table was silent. I smiled and introduced us blandly. Everyone was kind, but some were clearly confused—there was no paradigm for someone like me at this sort of table, I guess. Annie smiled kindly at me across the food. "I'm glad you're here," she whispered.

Father Matthew, a Jesuit priest from Illinois, was at the table with us. He genuinely seemed thrilled when he heard we were from outside the Catholic Church and then spent the evening chatting with us, making us feel welcome. It turned out that we had mutual friends, and I relaxed. We began to laugh and tell stories, and the table that had seemed so intimidating began to feel familiar. Perhaps this is one hidden reason that a shared table is at the center of our faith: we all relax when we're around a table.

At the end of the meal, our friend Bishop Q made a point of welcoming those of us from outside the Catholic faith to the weekend. He looked around the table at all of us, smiling like a man whose faraway dream has become reality.

We were sitting right across from him as he said, "You know, unity is something we already have between us," he said to me. "Because of Jesus! We are a family. We just don't always walk in it like this—let alone enjoy it . . ." He paused and looked at Brian and Father Michael, deep in good conversation, heads together, and then at everyone else laughing around the table. ". . . yet."

On our way back to our pension, I stopped in front of a forbidding statue in the market square, Campo de' Fiori. Brian missed that I had stopped and kept walking. I was arrested by this statue of an ominous man with his hands clasping a thick book, his face shadowed by his hood, his eyes defiant straight toward the Vatican just beyond the square. Brian came back to me, and, from his trusty guidebook—always in hand—we quickly learned that this was philosopher Giordano Bruno, executed by the Church in the seventeenth century. Inscribed on the base of the towering statue: *To Bruno—the century predicted by him—here where the fire burned*. On the base of the statue were also large icons of other philosophers and theologians persecuted by the Catholic Church, including Wycliffe. Underneath the medallions was a relief of Bruno being burned at the stake at this very spot. The bustling piazza, surrounded by restaurants with white paper or red-checked tablecloths, populated with street performers and pickpockets, was also the site to honor martyrs for free thought, the ones who resisted the Church. We walked back to our room in silence.

The next afternoon, we caught a bus to Vatican City to tour St. Peter's Basilica with the group. The golden cathedral was luminous from within, and the smoke from candles curled upward into the light like rising prayers. I thought of our own church's folding chairs in the school gym with surprise longing. The stunning and awe-inspiring architecture, the historic beauty, only made me realize afresh how deeply Protestant I am at my core, how I would have jumped ship with the Reformers in a heartbeat, how I inherently distrusted the grandeur and the gold, the incense and the obvious displays of wealth and power often built on the backs of the poor.

"It is . . . impressive," Brian said, watching people crawl on their knees toward the altar, pausing to pray with each hitch.

I found my way to Michelangelo's Pieta at one of the side chapels. This impossibly young Mary draped in marble cloth, holding her crucified Son sprawled in her lap, caught my breath. The grieving mother's palpable devastation, how easily she held him as if the years of cradling Jesus when he was a child never left her. Among all of the gold and deep colors of the basilica, the cool blue-white marble kept my attention.

After we left the basilica, passing by the Swiss Guards in their Medici blue, red, and yellow stripes, I lay down on the stones of the square near the fountain to straighten my back for a moment. Looking up into the clear blue sky, past the gold and the marble and the relics and colonnades, my body ached for pine trees as much as for a bed.

As the day wound down, we thought about going back to the hotel. I was on the cusp of too much for the day already. But instead, we went around back to the Musei Vaticani to see the Sistine Chapel before calling it a night. Tomorrow we would have our papal audience at the Apostolic Palace and then enjoy the prayer vigil at the Circus Maximus. Brian recommended a return to the pension so that I could rest, but this was our only opportunity to see the famous ceiling in the chapel and I didn't want to miss it.

We began our pilgrimage with the crowd, shuffling from room to room to room. The artwork began to blur together, and I swallowed tears of exhaustion and pain. Brian wrapped his arm around me. I was weary of statues and tapestries. "I can't keep going," I admitted.

"I knew you were overdoing it today," Brian said. He settled me onto a bench and inquired of a docent if we were closer to the exit or the entrance for a getaway: it turned out we were dead center in the maze, and it would take either me walking or him carrying me for us to make it out. We began to trudge through the halls of ancient maps and frescoes, tapestries draped on the walls muffling the stone and our voices. The light grew dimmer with every step farther into the heart of the building. The museum halls were forbidding, and it felt like we would be walking here forever, suffocated by bygone worship.

All of a sudden, I didn't like it at the Vatican, not anymore. My physical discomfort and spiritual discomfort were being linked: I couldn't make my body take even one more step, and I was wondering how in the world would the apostles react to all of this if they were here among us right now? Would they recognize this glory as their humble, squabbling community? The unity that Bishop Q had spoken of last night felt far away from me in this place: I wasn't welcome to the bread and wine at this table; my body was falling apart in one of the world's loveliest places of worship. I felt bewildered and adrift. How had a Jewish rabbi carpenter who preached on hillsides and drank water from wells and touched lepers given rise to this sort of opulence?

Finally we made it to the chapel, the last stop before the exit corridor. We squeezed into the crowded room with everyone else whose heads were tipped up to the famous ceiling. I leaned up against Brian, and there, hidden in the crowd, disoriented and weary, I let myself cry as I had wanted to since St. Peter's.

I looked for some solace in the chapel—*Are you here, Spirit?*—but found none. Perhaps this isn't surprising given my state of mind. The almighty fresco behind the altar, the masterpiece of Michelangelo titled *The Last Judgment*, looked nothing like the God that I knew and loved. This wasn't the story I believed with my whole life.

The fresco was a scene of commotion and terror: the saints surrounding this version of Jesus holding up the proof of their salvation or their martyrdom as the damned writhed in horror in their descent. Jesus looked more like an impassive Greek god than the Jewish carpenter who showed up at the beach after his resurrection to cook breakfast for Peter and the others, who ate with sinners, who raised the dead, who spat in the dirt and put mud on the eyes of the blind to heal them, who wept outside of Lazarus' tomb, our *God With Us*.

As we stood there, I remembered a line from one of John's letters: "There is no fear in love. But perfect love drives out fear, because fear has to do with punishment."[*]

And yet I was also afraid. Perhaps I wasn't afraid of judgment as the original audiences may have been, but I was afraid—I could admit that. Even my angst was a ballast against my fear.

I was afraid that I would never walk without pain again. I was afraid of my future. I was afraid of losing my work and my voice, my vocation and my calling. I was afraid of my children growing up without the mother they once had. I was afraid of the unknown, I was afraid of never finding out what was wrong with me, and I was afraid of finding out at last. I was afraid of admitting how not-fine I was out loud. And I was afraid that this would be my life now.

Part of me wanted to stand up on the altar and preach like I had never preached before in my life—to tell the story of the Prodigal Son and about the wild, generous welcome of God, the God who lifts up his robes and sprints down the driveway just to throw his arms around you when you finally come home. I also wanted to lie down on the floor and take a nap.

Instead, I moved to the walls and sat down on a ledge with

[*] 1 John 4:18, NIV.

elderly people. A woman who was ninety if she was a day cried beside me, whispering quiet words to herself in a language I couldn't understand. This was her home, her story, her legacy: not mine perhaps.

I looked up at the ceiling and saw *The Creation of Man*— the famous image of God's energy and breath hurtling toward Adam's lethargy to bring him life. "See, I am here too," a familiar voice whispered in my heart. The colors were like spring, glowing from the ceiling in the darkness like a light source. There you are.

Brian and I left the chapel, his right arm around me holding me upright, my left hand in his left hand for support.

As we waited for a taxi, I remembered the woman singing into the night just two nights ago, the sharpness of artichokes, the warmth of the wine on my tongue. I remembered the evening light on the walls of Orvieto and the way it felt to stretch in bed after a good night's sleep. I remembered Father Matthew's warmth and welcome, Bishop Q's prayers, the kindness of those gathered at the table. I remembered the spires of home and the smell of jasmine in twisty streets here. I remembered that there is no fear in love.

Whatever was ahead, I could remember the energetic love of God reaching toward us, toward me, always.

CHAPTER 7

THE POPE AND ME

I'm sorry, you're not on the list," the man said. We were on the steps of the Apostolic Palace, pressed and scrubbed and ready to meet Pope Francis.

I turned to Brian and he raised his shaggy eyebrows. Bishop Q pressed in to compare his list and the gatekeeper's list, identifying gaps and names, pulling in favors, making phone calls to his contact on the inside. We stood to the side with our group. The men were in suits, and everyone who was entitled to a white collar was sporting it; I was wearing the aforementioned pantyhose with my black dress despite the hot June sun. We stood on the steep stairs to the right of the imposing doors, and the minutes kept passing. We were not on the list. Apparently we would not be entering the palace today or any other day. Brian shrugged. "This will be a good story to tell my mom—us Protestants, locked outside the palace." The part of me that was still conflicted about our presence here was almost relieved.

Father Matthew was there with us, and his name was, in fact, on the list. He could have walked through the tall doors at any moment, but he stayed there with us, patiently waiting. "Go on in, Father!" we said. "Your name is on the list! It's the Pope! Go!" but he remained with us. He didn't make much of a show about it, but he was resolute: as long as we were on this side of the door, he would stay on this side of the door. We began to making terrible jokes about being "left behind."

Just northeast of St. Peter's Basilica, the Apostolic Palace is the official residence of the Pope. Inside, there are the papal apartments, the offices for the Vatican, the museum, secret rooms of art that makes the Louvre look like an upstart, the Vatican library, and the Sistine Chapel we had toured the night before. Since the seventeenth century, every Pope has made his home here in this place. Father Matthew told us that Pope Francis was the first one to break with this tradition: he declined to stay in the papal apartments, preferring to stay in a small guest apartment with other people. Apparently when he walked into the official residence the first time, he exclaimed, "But there's room for three hundred people here!"* and immediately made plans to live in a less ostentatious home so that he could live a more normal life, connected to the community who also lives there. He was wary of being isolated in grandeur, away from the people he serves. Stories like this are why I stayed on the steps: some part of me believed that this Pope was authentic, not simply out for the perks and privileges of power.

We stood in a loose circle. The tiled stairs were full of people waiting to enter the tall bronze doors: for every ten people

* While writing this book, I Googled what Father Matthew told us on the steps, and it's legit. Here's a news article about it: https://www.telegraph.co.uk/news/world news/the-pope/10086876/Pope-Francis-shunned-official-papal-apartments-to-live -normal-life.html.

approaching the man with the master list, only one was admitted. Many more people showed up than were expected. Father Matthew brought us nearer to himself and began to pray: he prayed that if it was the will of God for us to be here, that we would together walk through the doors as one—united. He reminded God of their habit of opening doors that no man could shut, and then we prayed the Lord's Prayer together, our voices blending in our shared liturgy.

Bishop Q poked his head into our prayer circle. "Sorry to interrupt," he said, "but we're in. Let's go."

When we walked through the imposing doors, we entered a portico with tall columns and were directed to a flight of stairs. I squared my shoulders and began to climb. We walked up five flights of wide stone stairs, flanked by paintings and sculptures. We saw a glimpse of each floor as we climbed and craned our necks to see around hidden corners. Phil, one of the priests who had been at the dinner two nights ago, climbed with us. By the third turn, I was clutching the handrails and hauling myself upward, hand over hand; it wasn't elegant, but I was determined to keep climbing.

"It's a lovely room, very opulent," Phil told us. "There are frescoes for St. Clement on the ceiling, and the floor is art in and of itself."

"Oh, you've been here before?" I asked breathlessly. I wanted him to keep talking so that I could concentrate on his words instead of on the climb.

"A few times," he said modestly.

"Cool, what else should we know?" Brian asked.

"Well, it's called the Clementine Hall officially. It's quite old, and it's the room where the Pope hosts his private audiences. Every time I've been here before, there is a big gold and red velvet throne at one end where His Holiness will sit. It's usually on a tall dais so that when he sits down, he's still above our heads while he speaks, which is protocol, I believe. Sometimes there will be chairs around the edges of the room when he's meeting with his cardinals, but for folks like us, the chairs will be removed and we'll just stand. It will be a short meet and greet, I imagine. You'll enjoy it—it's very beautiful. And also, I mean, it *is* the Pope!"

His enthusiasm and warmth reopened my heart to this day. When we entered the room, everything was as he had said. The room was overwhelmingly beautiful and grand, tall ceilings filled with Renaissance art, but unlike the enclosed chapel of the previous night and the long, dark hallways of the Musei Vaticani, this hall was lit up with natural light from wide windows along an entire wall. I perked up immediately. We filed in with our group of about a hundred people and stood around the edges of the room. The crowds parted gradually so we could see the head of the room, and that's when I heard our friend gasp audibly.

"Look at the throne," he whispered in disbelief.

Instead of the anticipated gold and red velvet throne presiding on a high dais, there was something else entirely. One humble wooden chair. That's it. One plain chair, placed on the same floor upon which we stood without dais or carpet or ornament, all of it awaiting the Pope. I grinned. Perhaps it was a theological statement, or perhaps we weren't worthy of the good stuff. Or maybe it was a choice I understood—to stubbornly become less impressive in response to the pressure to impress.

When Pope Francis walked into the room, we all applauded.

We were mostly informal North Americans, and I still have no idea if that broke every protocol of the Vatican, but we managed to restrain whooping, so I'm going to call it a win for the North American Church. Everyone stood up a bit straighter in his presence. We smiled back at his warm smile, his arms spread wide to welcome us. He stood in front of his chair in his signature white robes, flanked by cardinals in black and red dress robes.

He welcomed us with warmth, acknowledging that we were all from different branches of the family tree but declaring that we were still a family, the family of God.

In that moment, I loved Pope Francis even as I struggled to feel I belonged in his official home.

I loved the stairs up to this room and I resented them for the climb. I loved the grandeur and I distrusted it. I loved the art around us and I resented it. I loved the rituals and then I wanted to bang a tambourine and dance in the chapels. I loved the incense and I needed fresh air.

I loved the stained glass and I wanted to throw a rock through the window. I lit candles while praying in tongues. I kneeled alongside pilgrims and then stood up in defiance. I hugged priests in collars and I worried that our new friendship could be seen as my complicity in the Church's residential school abuses. I loved the glorious statues that I wanted to tip over one second later.

I longed for the notion of unity even as I struggled to draw near to traditions and theology different from my own.

And yet here we all were: an act of faith in our bruised unity, embodied.

Pope Francis began to pray the Lord's Prayer, and we all

joined in, each speaking our own languages. He looked up at us after our cacophony settled into a combined "Amen," earnest in his gaze, and through a translator he said, "You have heard it said, 'come home to Rome' from us. But there is no need for you to come home—you are at home where you are.* We are one already."

I felt like he looked right at me. Maybe that's just a trick of my memory. Maybe everyone felt like he looked at them in that bold statement. We were home and we were not at home, but we were all welcome.

He never did sit down.

Pope Francis began to walk around the room, shaking hands and offering blessings. As he drew nearer to us, I gulped and looked across the room. Both Pastor Ed and Bishop Q were grinning at me and waggling their fingers in a discreet wave, their whole expressions communicating their delight as if to say, *Isn't this fun?*

Eventually he made his way to us through the crowd, reaching out to shake our hands. First Brian's, and then he took my hand in his and smiled at me.

"Hi," I said with a smile. "Thank you for this."

"Bless you," he said.

"Thank you," I said.

---

* I have this entire paragraph written down in my journal from that day. When we came back to the pension that evening, I wanted to make sure I didn't forget this in particular. But when I went to check the remarks on the Vatican's website, they did not appear in the Pope's "official remarks" from that day. Perhaps it wasn't official record since they were spoken after the prayer. I checked with other people who were there at the event, though, and they all remember hearing this phrase—"there is no need for you to come home"—so I feel confident to include it here.

"Pray for me?" he asked.

"I will," I said. "I will."

He patted our clasped hands with his other hand and nodded while looking into my eyes. The photographer's camera flashed as we smiled at each other, our hands still entwined.

After our audience with Pope Francis, we were led back outside. We walked back down the steps where we had been stranded just an hour before. In the crush of people, I was separated from Brian. He was nowhere to be found. I did find Annie, Bishop Q's wife, and we leaned together against one of the massive and cool stone columns in the portico, talking about the morning's audience and our impressions so far. She marveled at my pantyhose choice in June's heat. I wasn't worried—Brian would find me eventually, and he's easy to spot in a crowd since he's a head taller than everyone else.

Ten minutes later, I caught sight of him standing among all of the people at the base of the steps, and I called his name. He turned toward me slowly in a daze, looking disoriented. I waved and he made his way over to us, shaking his head as if to clear it.

"Did you see me talking to those two priests?" he asked slowly.

"No, not really," I said. "I just saw you. What's going on? You look like you've seen a ghost."

"I'm not entirely sure I didn't just meet two angels," he said. "That was . . . something."

"What happened?" I asked.

He told me that on his way down the stairs, he ran into two priests—literally. He bumped right into them from behind, causing both of them to stumble forward. The priests turned around, and their faces broke into huge grins while Brian apologized profusely as the Canadian he has become.

"You're as tall as us!" one exclaimed in a thick Scottish brogue. The two priests were just as tall as Brian when they straightened up, the three of them towering over the crowd. "Any chance you're a priest? Then you can be part of our Tall, Handsome Priest Club!"

Brian laughed at their enthusiastic welcome and struck up a conversation as he often does with strangers.* Their names were Harold and Theo—Harold was originally from Scotland and Theo was from Alberta, the province right beside ours where they both now made their home. The priests were delighted to find someone "from back home" all the way in Rome. It seemed providential to bump into a couple of Canadians in this place of all places.

"Honestly, it was just nice to chat with a couple of easygoing guys after all that formality upstairs," Brian told me.

"Were they invited by the same group as us?" I asked.

"That's what I asked," Brian said. "Theo said no one invited them, and they 'sensed God wanted them to be here.' So they came."

I blinked. "They just . . . came . . . all the way to Rome . . . because they thought . . . God wanted them here. Oh, Lord, they must be charismatics like us."

---

* You remember the story with the jug of milk in the Walmart. Story of my life.

"That's what I said to them!" Brian said. "Sure enough, they told me that they try to keep the appointments God makes. And after that conversation, I think I believe them."

"Tell me everything," I said. And he did.

As they chatted and got to know each other a bit, Harold turned to Theo and said, "Are you sensing it too?"

Theo nodded at him with a smile. They both turned to Brian and asked if he had ever heard of the phrase "word of knowledge."

This was familiar to both of us, of course. The phrase "word of knowledge" is from the first letter written by the Apostle Paul to the Church in Corinth. In one section of the letter, he tells the Church that he does not want them to be ignorant of the "gifts of the Spirit."

There are different kinds of gifts, but the same Spirit distributes them. There are different kinds of service, but the same Lord. There are different kinds of working, but in all of them and in everyone it is the same God at work. Now to each one the manifestation of the Spirit is given for the common good. To one there is given through the Spirit a message of wisdom, to another a message of knowledge by means of the same Spirit, to another faith by the same Spirit, to another gifts of healing by that one Spirit, to another miraculous powers, to another prophecy, to another distinguishing between spirits, to another speaking in different kinds of tongues, and to still another the interpretation of tongues. All these are the work of one and the same Spirit, and he distributes them to each one, just as he determines. *

* 1 Corinthians 12:4–11, NIV.

In our faith tradition, we had been taught that a message of knowledge—or, more commonly for those of us raised on the King James, *a word* of knowledge—was a "supernatural revelation of information pertaining to a person of an event, given for a specific purpose, usually having to do with an immediate need."* It's one part prophetic, one part discernment, all Spirit-led.

Now, Brian and I had had experiences with the practice of these gifts that ranged from the genuine blessing to the cringe-worthy nightmare. In our lives as charismatic believers within a context that adored prosperity, we had both received a "word of knowledge" from a well-meaning friend or church leader or fellow worshipper who was so wildly off base that it was laughable.

Even though I had experienced some brokenness or awkwardness around this practice, I still deeply believed in it. I have experienced the goodness of it too many times to doubt it now. Among the veiled manipulation and weirdness, I have also encountered believers with a word of knowledge at a key moment in my life which resonated deeply, as if the words of the other person rang a bell that had already been there in my soul.

There are too many moments to name, but one that comes to mind to share with you happened during one of the darkest and most grief-stricken moments of my life. I was about twenty-five years old at the time, so it's been a while. I was at church, our church, even though everything in me wanted to be back home

* The Spirit-Filled Life Bible commentary for this passage, accessed on Bible Gateway, July 2, 2018.

in our Texas bungalow, recovering from the miscarriage we had experienced only a few days prior.

We had no children, and this was yet another loss, my third. It was a difficult miscarriage, painful and drawn-out over weeks, culminating in a short labor and a lonely good-bye. The entire time that I was losing that baby, there was an accusation in my head toward God.

I kept repeating over and over, like a prayer or a mantra toward God, "You have forgotten me. You don't see me. You have forgotten me. You have forgotten me."

I was deep into deconstruction at the time, all of the edifices I had once built for God were crashing around me, and this was what felt like the final blow to my prosperity gospel word-of-faith paper castle of knowing God. I had done everything right: prayed the prayers, confessed the confessions, sung the songs, checked every box on every well-intentioned list. And yet still I was childless, still I was grieving. In a tradition built on the answered prayers and the victory, I was floundering to find myself as part of the company of the unanswered prayers, and to my eyes, God had disappeared.

I was forgotten. I was unseen. If God did not answer my prayers in the way that I thought prayers should be answered, perhaps everything I knew about God was wrong. So it wasn't only the miscarriage and the loss—although that was enough— it was also the loss of God.

As I sat in church that day, I couldn't bring myself to sing the songs anymore. The mantra persisted God-ward; as everyone else sang praises, I was in a loop of "You have forgotten me. You don't see me. You have forgotten me. You don't see me."

An older woman in our church who was only an acquaintance, not a friend, came to me at the end of the service. I had seen her watching me as I refused to stand and sing and, God forgive me, I was certain she was judging me. I had already been on the receiving end of correction a time or seven for my inability to behave as a proper pastor's wife.

But instead, she kneeled down at my feet and said gently, "Sarah, I have a word of knowledge from God for you. May I share it?"

Now, I don't know if you've ever found yourself in this situation, but it can go one of two ways. And as I said, I had experienced both, and in that moment I was inclined to think it would be another experience to chalk up to the kookiness of some of my brethren, a word to be endured and forgotten quickly. Honestly? There was nothing I wanted less than to hear this woman's "word of knowledge" for me—I was suspicious it would be a veiled rebuke of my lack of singing that morning.

But being a woman and a Canadian, of course I said, "Yes, please tell me your word."

This woman leaned in and took my hands. She began, "I was watching you this morning."

I thought, *Yes, I know, dear.*

She said, "As I watched you, I heard God give me a word for you. God asked me to walk over here to you and tell you this: *You are not forgotten.*"

You are not forgotten.

She continued, "You are not forgotten, and God sees you. I turned to Isaiah 49, and here, these words are for you, my dear."

Can a mother forget the baby at her breast
and have no compassion on the child she has borne?
Though she may forget,
I will not forget you!
*See, I have engraved you on the palms of my hands . . .**

Even if your mother forgets, I will not forget you.

I thought of the small babe we had wrapped in a tea towel just days before. I thought of the name we had given that small one. I thought of how the whole world would never know them, but I knew them, and how I would never forget. From this vantage point, years and years later, I know that that instinct was true: I have never forgotten. That child, just as the four that I lost and the four that live, is engraved on me.

Never forgotten.

I have never gotten over that moment, that word of knowledge, and I hope I never do. My mantra was disrupted, and I had a new path to walk, a path I still walk to this day. If God had not forgotten me—and clearly God had not—and yet I was still part of the company of the unanswered prayers, perhaps that meant that I had misunderstood something about God. Perhaps the problem wasn't God; perhaps the problem was the God I had created and the God I had been given.

This was not my only experience with words of knowledge. I have dozens of stories of fellow believers who discern God's voice with me and for me. So I do still believe in words of knowledge. I do believe the Spirit can speak directly to our

* Isaiah 49:15–16, NIV.

circumstances and our lives through the words of our fellow believers. I believe we can serve as gateways or conduits for one another to hear the Spirit, that discerning God's voice can be communal.

But Brian was a little less sold. My own unhealthy experiences with words of knowledge were mostly benign and inflicted no real, lasting damage—he had witnessed more serious spiritual abuse in that language and was much more wary.

He has told me stories of vulnerable women who were told they were possessed, that they needed an exorcism, which resulted in abuse and great damage to their mental health. He has never forgotten witnessing this as a child. He has told me stories of people using the notion of "words of knowledge" to manipulate people to their will, to make them behave the way they want, to isolate vulnerable people. Leaders who claimed a "word of knowledge" positioned themselves as above critique— nothing makes Brian head for the door faster now. And he has firsthand experience with people claiming a "word of knowledge" when really they were simply wanting their opinion or preference baptized.

My positive experiences with a word of knowledge far outweighed any negative experiences. Brian was not so fortunate. He was distrustful and wary of the language itself, let alone the practice. Because of his background, he has never been one to surrender his own discernment to someone else's prophetic urges.

Perhaps it was the incongruousness of a couple of tall priests from Scotland and Alberta talking about the word of knowledge that disarmed him that day. Perhaps it was the place and the unusual experiences of our morning. Perhaps it was the Holy Spirit. But either way, despite his usual distrust, he found himself laughing at their earnest question.

"Of course, I've heard of a word of knowledge! I'm charismatic from a Pentecostal background, after all. I've just never heard a couple of priests use the phrase!" And he welcomed them to speak into his life with more curiosity than conviction.

With very little fanfare or formality, the two priests began to tell him about his own life.

There was no way that they could have known the details they were sharing—they talked to him about his work, his background, his training, his longings, his vocation. They told him about his own life in this moment and gently offered words of clarity about his prayers and his hopes. Brian knew he was in the presence of something powerful unfolding. How could they know these things about him? How did they know what he needed to hear so clearly? He wept openly as they spoke to him. They placed their hands on his shoulders and prayed for him, simply and sincerely, asking God to sift their words and reveal to all of them if they were mistaken.

"Then what happened?" I asked.

"They disappeared. I mean, they left," he said. "Right when I heard you call my name, they said good-bye. I looked at you, and when I looked back, they were gone into the crowd. Sarah, they told me everything that led us here and offered such clarity to me about my own questions with God. It was . . . I don't even know what to call it."

When he finished telling me about it, I had goose bumps. It

reminded me of when Jesus encountered a woman at the well in Samaria. It's a beautiful story*—the longest recorded conversation between Jesus and anyone in Scripture—in which he tells the woman about her own life even though she had never met him before. Even though the disciples are scandalized—Jesus, alone with a woman, and a Samaritan woman at that! She returns to her village and tells everyone, "Come see this man, he told me everything I ever did!" and many people from the village began to follow Jesus because of her testimony.

"I hope we run into them again," he said. "I need to know that it really happened. I'd like to know that they are real guys. I can't believe this."

"Out of all the places and people where I expected a mystical encounter with God, it wasn't here," I admitted.

Brian took me back to our pension near Piazza Navona. The prayer vigil was scheduled for that afternoon at Circus Maximus rather than St. Peter's Square. Given our morning of climbing stairs, I was in too much pain to go, but after the encounter with Harold and Theo, Brian was quite eager to attend. Besides, I wasn't keen to go anyway. The idea of a Catholic prayer vigil didn't sound like my kind of place to encounter Jesus, so I fell asleep and he slipped out, taking the bus to the Circus.

When he came back to the pension hours later, I was awake and hungry, but Brian was practically floating three feet off the ground.

* You can read this story in John 4. And when you're done, go read a feminist literary commentary on that passage to love it even more.

"I think I just got a glimpse of what heaven is going to be like," he said.

At the Circus Maximus, more than thirty thousand pilgrims from 120 countries had come together to pray and celebrate the renewal from fifty years before and its ongoing impact worldwide today. Every nation was represented: people wore their traditional clothing, waved their flags, banged on tambourines, danced, spoke in tongues.

Three hours before the service even began, the crowd was singing spontaneously together in the sunshine. Brian was sitting in the first row, right in front of the Pope, who was flanked by two women rather than his cardinals. The stage backdrop was an enormous banner declaring *Jesus Is Lord* over and over, in dozens of languages.

"If I hadn't seen it with my own eyes, I wouldn't have believed it," he told me. "When the Pope arrived, we started to sing that old Latin American song *'Vive Jesús, El Señor'*— you know how much I love that song.* We straight-up had old-school praise and worship. I saw cardinals in their little red hats with their arms raised, singing 'Oceans.'†

"The Pope had his hands up and open too during worship— like a Pentecostal—and he seemed happy and utterly at home with us. I mean, it was so unreal. Pentecostals, Catholics, Anglicans, Presbyterians, us—all of us just singing our hearts out together. The two ladies beside the Pope were on their knees,

* Little-known fact about Brian: he speaks Spanish and lived in Mexico City for a time.
† "Oceans" by Hillsong UNITED (2013) was a very popular worship song at that time.

praying in tongues, and he was just swaying between them like he was comfortable with all of it. When he preached, he called the renewal movement a 'current of grace' and said that this moment is a 'reconciled diversity.'"

The Pope preached a message that left Brian hollering in his seat, proclaiming that this renewal, this current of grace, was for us all, not just for the Catholic Church, "walking together, working together, loving each other, and together seeking to explain our differences and seeking agreement, but on the way! If we stay put, without walking together, we will never, ever reach agreement because the Spirit wants us walking.*

"Is this a work that was born . . . Catholic? No. It was born ecumenical!" Pope Francis declared while the crowd cheered. "It was born ecumenical because it is the Holy Spirit that creates unity and the same Holy Spirit that gave the inspiration for it to be thus!"

I felt the sting of my own pridefulness as Brian shared about the vigil. I regretted my choice. I had thought that because I had been through a process of deconstruction and rebuilding that I was settled once again. But it turned out that I was just as prideful now, just as certain that I had the market cornered on the Spirit's movement and presence. I was still convinced I wouldn't hear from God in Rome, I was sure Jesus wouldn't meet with us here, I was certain that the Spirit was far from this place and tradition. And instead, at every turn, I was being challenged in that notion, being asked to open myself up to the

---

* You can read the Pope's full address from the Circus Maximus Golden Jubilee celebration at https://press.vatican.va/content/salastampa/en/bollettino/pubblico/2017/06/03/170603g.html.

possibility of being surprised by God yet again. I began to get ready for supper, as silent as Brian was exuberant. For all my talk about my openness to the Spirit, he was the one who had gone, he was the one who was having the mystical experiences, and I was not. I wasn't jealous—that wasn't it. But I was disoriented: in our marriage, I'm the one with the woo-woo spirituality; he's the steady studier. Our roles were being reversed, but it wasn't because there was only enough Spirit for one of us here; it was because I stubbornly refused to believe that God could meet with me here, in this place, with these people.

"I thought of my mother and my grandmother a lot today," Brian said later that night over our dinner with friends. "I wish they both could have seen this."

We spent the remainder of the day with the group, talking over a meal and marveling over the messages. We told stories and asked questions; we ordered another bottle of wine. New people joined our wide table, including a priest from Florida named Bill and his wife, Theresa; a pastor from a megachurch in Houston and his media team; a pastor from Argentina. We dragged more café tables over, extending the table with each new arrival. It turned out we wanted to be friends with all of the people who had seemed so far away a short time ago. We were being woven together, and I resolved to stay more open. Father Matthew caught my eye at the end of the table and grinned.

CHAPTER 8

MIRACLES IN ROME

The next morning, we debated staying at the pension and skipping Mass. It was Pentecost Sunday.* Most of our group elected to skip the Mass at St. Peter's Square as a gentle form of protest because we were not allowed to partake of the Eucharist. Unity and reconciled diversity and ecumenicalism seemed so real yesterday but felt far away in the morning as one after another of our Protestant companions chose sightseeing over being shut out from the Eucharist—a choice that, let's be honest, I understood and affirmed. As I said earlier, the table's openness and welcome is deeply important to me. It's not a reward for good behavior, it's an invitation to shared practice, to the family. Even though part of me wanted to make the same peaceful protest, we decided to go to Mass in an act of faith, in solidarity with yesterday's dream of unity. We decided there was a witness to standing there in the crowd, barred from the table but present anyway.

---

* Pentecost Sunday is the seventh Sunday after Easter. On that day, Christians remember and mark the story as told in Acts 2:1–31 when the Holy Spirit descended upon the followers of Jesus who were in an Upper Room together. This moment is considered the birth of the Church. It's one of my favorite stories.

"I think we need to be there," Brian said as we walked toward the Vatican again. "I'm not entirely sure why. I just know we're supposed to be there."

"Look at you, being all 'hearing from Jesus,'" I teased. "Who knew Rome would do the trick?"

On our way there, my body seized up again, and I sat down on the curb. My spine still felt twisted, and my muscles were unable to bear the weight any longer. Beggars were everywhere in the press of people above me. Everyone walked past us on his or her way to Rome. I looked up at the crowd of legs, the children staring at the outstretched hands. It stank down near the gutter: sweat and sour food. Bizarrely, I caught sight of Father Matthew near us—he was crouched down on the curb near me. I tugged on Brian's pant leg and motioned toward the priest.

"There's Father Matthew," I said. I should have been surprised to encounter him by chance here, but I had ceased being surprised. I was beginning to believe Brian's priest friends: we were all keeping the appointments that God had set here. Everywhere I looked from the curb, I saw the priests, praying for the poor, filling up their cups while tourists passed them by. A woman cried out blessings from the street gutter, and we filled her tin cup. Brian snagged Father Matthew as he rose from his conversation, lifted me to my feet so that I wouldn't be trampled, and together we walked toward St. Peter's Square.

When we arrived, it was absolute chaos. No one was getting past the beefed-up security. The square was full, and every road was jammed with people. That morning there had been a terrorist attack in London, and security was on even higher alert, locking down every corner, setting up metal detectors at every entrance.

There was no way we would find our way into the Mass, no way we would find our group in this ocean of humanity. We stood in the bright sunshine and wondered if this had been a waste of time.

"Let's wait a bit longer," I said. "Maybe if we walk around the perimeter we will find someone from our group or a way inside."

Less than a minute later, I saw the couple from Florida whom we had met the night before. By now, I had given up being surprised that in the crush of almost fifty thousand souls, we kept finding the exact people we needed to find. "It's Bill and Theresa. Let's see if they know what's going on," I said. They were facing us, talking to two tall priests.

"They're talking to Harold and Theo!" Brian said in amazement. There they were—Harold and Theo. They were real after all. Brian introduced us all. They had somehow found themselves standing beside Bill and Theresa earlier and struck up a conversation.

We began to talk with everyone about the crowd of people and the unlikely chance of our getting inside the square for Mass, trying to make plans for what to do next. We debated making an attempt on the other side of the square in case the line for security was perhaps lessened. We wondered if our badges from Bishop Q would get us in the door. Meanwhile, Harold and Theo were quietly talking between themselves; I assumed they were making their own plans while we made ours. I held myself gingerly, feeling like I was about to fall over, grimacing through a hip joint spasm, adjusting my posture every three seconds to try to find some measure of relief.

Theo turned to me and said, "Sarah, Harold and I sense God wants you to experience healing. Is there something going on in your body?"

Brian's jaw fell open. Father Matthew beamed.

I told them that I had been in a car accident a few months before and that I was still struggling. I had grown used to people's curiosity at my odd habits to accommodate my battered body, and so I shrugged off their interest. I downplayed the severity of my pain and always minimized my injuries. I told them nothing specific, only that it had been a hard few months. I don't know why I had—and still have—such an aversion to being honest about pain. Brian's theory is that it's cultural: Canadians could be going through hell but when asked, will only say that "it's been a bit of a day."

He stepped in with his revived faith in the supernatural, telling the group that I was not being exactly truthful: I was in constant debilitating pain and it was only getting worse.

"Can we pray for you?" Harold asked. His eyes were kind, and, like Brian before me, I trusted him almost instantly.

"Yes," I said slowly. I didn't like the attention, I didn't know what they would say to me, but I said yes anyway.

The group formed a circle around me, with Brian at my back, Father Matthew and Bill and Theresa at my sides, Harold and Theo to my face. Each one asked if they could touch me, and after I consented, they all placed their hands very gently on my shoulders or on my upper arms, Brian's hands at the back of my neck.

Harold began to pray with such intimacy, such authority, such tenderness, it felt like encountering an old friend. Theo began to pray as well. Together, they were weaving their prayers with silence, as if they were listening for a response. We waited, tarrying like Quakers in expectation of the voice of God.

Then Harold began to name some of my injuries.

"Your spine," he said and paused. "Move, Lord."

"Your vertebrae here . . . move, Lord."

"Your neck . . . move, Lord."

"Your left hip . . . move, Lord."

At his words, I felt a cooling liquid sensation rising up from my tailbone, through my hips, up through my spine, reaching the base of my neck.

I turned around to ask Brian how in the world he was pouring cool water *up* my spine, but he was empty-handed, staring back at me, his hazel eyes round. Something was happening. What was going on?

The pleasant coolness wrapped around every joint in my spine, moving slowly up through my injuries. I felt my vertebrae rotating like gears turning in my spine, one by one, moving in response to Harold's words.

Harold opened his eyes and looked right at me. "I see your bones, especially your spine, like it is a xylophone and it has been twisted and torn and fractured, discordant. But God is right now realigning it. By the end of today, your spine will be realigned. Your body is meant to be a testimony of God's healing, Sarah. This is the beginning right now, but this isn't the end. This won't be all of it, not yet. It will be complete in God's time."

At that, everything that had been hurting in my spine and hips simply released its grip and disappeared. The pain evaporated like a bad dream upon waking.

I lifted my arms above my head and tipped my face to the sky. I felt free. The cool sensation lifted, and I dropped my arms, rolling my shoulders. Everyone had their eyes on me.

"I think . . . I think my back is healed," I said. And promptly burst into noisy, snotty tears. Brian wrapped his arms around me.

"Really?" he asked, looking into my eyes intently. "Slow down and don't jump to conclusions. Really?"

"Yes." I nodded. "My back is fine, really fine. I feel . . . good. Like everything was washed away."

He bowed his head and rested his forehead against mine. "Praise God," he whispered in a moment. "Praise God."

Minutes or hours later—who can remember?—Father Matthew led us through the crowd to an official at the gate so that we could enter for Mass and, in the greatest miracle of Rome, we found ourselves waved through security, welcomed. Harold and Theo bade us a joyful good-bye and said they preferred to stay outside with the crowd. We pressed into the square and found a patch of shade under the colonnades surrounding the square with those in wheelchairs or with small children. We were still disoriented, overwhelmed, unable to realize what had just happened.

The ornate service, filled with important people in robes, was as the rest of our Protestant group had suspected: a traditional Catholic service in a language we didn't understand. I listened quietly to the cadence of Latin. My eyes fell on Father

Matthew, here in Rome for a moment that was meaningful to him. I began to put myself in his sensible shoes, imagining this moment from his perspective: to listen to the Mass in St. Peter's Square, presided over by one's own Pope. What a memory for him, the stuff to cherish for a lifetime. I was happy to witness this moment for our new friend.

After the sermon and chants, when the Eucharist began, I turned to Father Matthew and brightly said, "Away you go!" motioning for him to head toward the Basilica to join the queue of priests eligible to receive the Eucharist that morning. It was time for the big moment, the Body and Blood of Christ to be given to him in this place. I wasn't even resentful any longer—this didn't feel like my table—and I was cheerful on his behalf.

"It's time," Brian said and smiled at him. "We'll wait for you here."

Father Matthew looked at me patiently, as if I were a small child who had misunderstood the moment completely: "Sarah, I won't partake of the Eucharist now. Not if you and Brian can't also partake."

"Father Matthew!" I was shocked. "You can't be serious."

Brian joined me in my protest. "We are fine, we promise. You go—it's all good."

"This is the mother ship! You're a Jesuit priest, this is Rome, that there is your Pope! Go on!" I said more urgently.

He refused again. "My conscience won't allow it," he said. "We must take every opportunity to stand in solidarity with each other, don't you think? While you are not welcome at the Table with me, I cannot eat from the Table. Either it's for all of us or it's for none of us."

Brian and I looked at each other. We felt terrible. If we hadn't come to Mass, he would have perhaps been able to partake. Because we were here, he was compelled to stay with us and abstain from what could only have been a once-in-a-lifetime opportunity of great spiritual import for him.

"Father Matthew," we said. "We release you! We release you from this commitment to unity for just today. No one will judge you for this—we want you to enter into this special moment with your Church. We know that you are with us in spirit—we honor that, but we genuinely *want* you to have this experience."

He smiled at us, unmoved and gentle in his defiance of our pleas. It was as if we had implored him to sprout a new limb, he was that incapable of going against his convictions.

"How about this . . . ," he finally said as a concession. "Why don't we get together with Bishop Q and the group later this evening for our own homemade Eucharist? I'll even get the English translation of the sermon this morning and we'll have an ecumenical Pentecost celebration of the Eucharist tonight. All of us."

We agreed to his proposal and left Mass with all its pomp and pageantry behind us.

We could not even speak of what had happened earlier with Harold and Theo. Every time we tried to talk about it, words failed us—we were wonderstruck. Every ten steps, Brian would say, "How is your back now?" and I would twist back and forth and say, "Fine. I think it's really properly fine."

We lay down beside each other in our bed that afternoon and

slept like babies, exhausted by a world that was entirely new to us. We had no idea what to expect next, filled with unsteady awe.

I woke up from our nap and sprang out of the bed, Brian watching me like a hawk to see if I would wince or stumble, eventually satisfied that I was moving easily. We rode the bus and walked to Bishop Q's hotel room near the Vatican for the homemade Eucharist, eager to see our friends with our news. Upon our arrival, we were shown up to the bishop and Annie's room along with Father Matthew, Bishop Ed, and a few priests from our evening dinner of a few nights before.

When we walked in, I heard a now-familiar Scottish voice say my name in surprise. Harold and Theo. Here they were, again, of all places. They had met Phil, the same priest who had walked up the stairs with us at the Apostolic Palace the day before, and he had invited them to join him at a small Pentecost Eucharist with his friends. They had simply said yes and followed him here to us.

We embraced in disbelief—why did our paths keep crossing with these two random priests from Alberta? With the addition of Harold and Theo, we were now twelve souls in the upper room across the street from the Vatican on Pentecost Sunday.

There was a small heel of bread on a room service table and a bottle of table red wine. We sprawled on the bed and in the chairs around the room. I looked at their faces and smiled—just three days ago, I had sat at a table with most of these men and felt pressure to impress. Now they were friends. We had gotten to know them beyond their collars and their titles: it turned out that they were humble, quick to prayer and laughter; they had an easy way of embodying the Gospel that felt seamless to me. There was no boundary between the life of the Spirit and their real walking-around life. They cared for others without performance. They were grieved by injustice, committed to repentance and reconciliation. I simply loved them all.

Father Matthew began by reading the morning's Pentecost homily from Pope Francis. He cleared his throat and in a comical attempt at the Pope's accent said, "Today concludes the Easter season, the fifty days that, from Jesus' resurrection to Pentecost, are marked in a particular way by the presence of the Holy Spirit." His mimicry was so horrible, it was hilarious, and we all burst out in laughter. He beamed like a kid—even Father Matthew likes to be the funny one now and again.

We settled down eventually and he began again, this time in his regular Midwestern voice. Pope Francis' sermon was a continuation of the theme of the weekend, a meditation on how the Spirit makes us a new people and creates in each of us a new heart.* As he read, the room's edges began to soften. The Pope had preached about Pentecost's gift of unity, and he warned us against two temptations:

The first was the temptation of diversity without unity. Pope Francis said, "This happens when we want to separate, when we take sides and form parties, when we adopt rigid and air-tight positions, when we become locked into our own ideas and ways of doing things, perhaps even thinking that we are better than others, or always in the right, when we become so-called

---

* You can read the Pope's full homily—which I highly recommend—here: https://w2 .vatican.va/content/francesco/en/homilies/2017/documents/papa-francesco_20170604 _omelia-pentecoste.html.

'guardians of the truth.' When this happens, we choose the part over the whole, belonging to this or that group before belonging to the Church. We become avid supporters for one side, rather than brothers and sisters in the one Spirit. We become Christians of the 'right' or the 'left,' before being on the side of Jesus, unbending guardians of the past or the avant-garde of the future before being humble and grateful children of the Church."

And the second temptation is unity without diversity because "Here, unity becomes uniformity, where everyone has to do everything together and in the same way, always thinking alike. Unity ends up being homogeneity and no longer freedom."

The priests in the room wiped their eyes. I said, "Yes! come on, come through!" a few times, like the tent revival Pentecostal I still am at heart, when Father Matthew read, ". . . ask for a heart that feels that the Church is our Mother and our home, an open and welcoming home where the manifold joy of the Holy Spirit is shared."

At the end, he paused and took a deep breath before reading the benediction: "The Holy Spirit is the fire of love burning in the Church and in our hearts, even though we often cover him with the ash of our sins. Let us ask him: 'Spirit of God, Lord, who [dwells] in my heart and in the heart of the Church, guiding and shaping her in diversity, come! Like water, we need you to live. Come down upon us anew, teach us unity, renew our hearts and teach us to love as you love us, to forgive as you forgive us.'"

Silence fell. Father Matthew quietly said, "Amen," and set down the piece of paper from which he had been reading, tapping it once with his finger as punctuation.

It was all there in that sermon. Everything I had wrestled with since our arrival—I had a rightful suspicion of unity without diversity, a distrust of it, but I had inadvertently given in to the flip side, of diversity without unity. I had forgotten that the Holy Spirit is shared. In that quiet room of twelve disciples, I wanted, all over again, to be on the side of Jesus, not on the side of my tradition or my deconstruction or my future wanderings. I wanted to receive the gift of Pentecost, the gift of unity and power and a new heart, in hope and grace, faith and fire. I opened my hands wide, letting my body tell the story of my soul in that moment.

We sang "Spirit of the Living God," an old revival hymn, together. I hadn't heard this song since I was a kid, but the words felt familiar in my mouth:

> *Spirit of the living God,*
> *Fall afresh on me.*
> *Melt me, mould me, fill me, use me.*
> *Spirit of the living God,*
> *Fall afresh on me.*

Pastor Ed stood up at the room service table and began our Eucharist for misfits. It was both familiar and unfamiliar to us—Pastor Ed was our bridge between our Low Church convictions and the High Church rituals. We were reconciled to one another in that room: a precious and tender-hearted Jesuit, absolutely anointed Anglicans, charismatic Episcopalians, faithful steady Catholics, and now us two with our complicated new expressions of North American Christianity inexplicably present, who cried through it all. I look back on it now, and it seems bathed in holiness, the greatest miracle of Rome.

I used to think that the Holy Spirit would show up in great and grand displays of power. I had been taught and trained to expect the Big Move of God, the Big Revival, the Big Display. But instead, even though I had experienced what seemed to be a supernatural healing that very day, the miracle of us all there in that room loomed larger than any of it.

This was a humble and ordinary miracle—bread, wine, singing together, Scripture read in community, prayer, unity and diversity together. It felt like we were mere breaths away from a mighty rushing wind and tongues of fire: I would not have been one bit surprised.

We sang the doxology with breath that tasted of the blood of Christ. Everything in this moment was familiar and yet the birth of something brand-new.

Afterward, we paused. It was as if the presence among us was waiting. We sat quietly in the tangible divine, waiting. I breathed in the air of it, aware of the old word we used to use for these moments, a *stirring* to describe the activity of God on the darkness, sensing its rightness.

Then someone in the room asked aloud if they could pray for me.

Why me? I have no idea. I can't imagine that my needs outweighed theirs on that evening. I was reluctant to take more than I had already been given—I was being greedy with the Spirit, wasn't I? I wanted to deflect, to redirect, to shrink away, but instead I fought my instinct to hide and I stood up.

Annie pressed a tissue into my hands, and when I pressed it

to my face, it came away covered in mascara. I stood on the tile floor, and all of the men gathered around me, Annie by my side.

They prayed the roof off that room, affirming me as called and gifted and ready for healing. They blessed me in my work, commissioned me to write and to preach and to lead the Church. They prayed for Brian and his own work and our vocation together both in the world and in our home.

Pastor Ed confirmed the healing that I had experienced with Harold and Theo earlier that morning, and then gently he said, "Now, let's pray for your mind, Sarah. Let's pray for God to present and minister somehow to your anxiety and mental health."

I had not told him about these things, but by now I had stopped being surprised. He prayed for me, and I held up my hands, palms facing heaven, wondering how I could hold such embarrassment of goodness. I could feel Brian's hands on my shoulders as he stood behind me, his body hot to the touch. Even if none of this was true, even if I didn't believe it later, even if I needed to unpack and wrestle with each moment eventually, I believed it in that moment, and it was so much more than enough.

Theo paused and said quietly from my left, "You may need to remember this prayer, this moment, in the months ahead, Sarah. I believe you will need to remember this."

Bishop Q stepped in front of me. "Sarah, you have walked these streets in suffering," he said. I dropped my head, closing my eyes at the light.

"You walked these streets in suffering; you suffered with each step. If you hadn't limped through Rome, if you hadn't wept through Italy in pain, you would have missed seeing Italy with the eyes of the grieving and the hurting and the left out. But God is saying, you will go home leaping all as a sign of his grace and his power still available to us all. This is not over for you. Not yet."

At those words, I lifted my head up and looked at him. He nodded. I nodded. Something seemed understood beyond words. This was only a beginning of a healing.

The circle broke, and we all began to laugh shakily, trying to transition from wherever we had been to where we were going next. Anne gave me more tissues.

Phil came to me and pulled me aside. I imagine I looked like a drenched cat, soggy with tears, still shaking my head in disbelief at all of this, unable to understand it but believing nonetheless. God was doing something miraculous; it was improbable and completely ordinary.

Phil took a small vial from his inside jacket pocket. Tipping the vial over, he anointed the fingers on one of his hands lightly, then he set down the bottle and took my hand with his other hand. Slowly he stretched out his hand to my face and deliberately drew the sign of the cross on my forehead, consecrating me. Quietly he said, "I mark you, Sarah, with the holy cross—to seal the work of Christ done in you on this day. I seal it in the name of Jesus and with the power of the Spirit."

PART III

◈

If there is anywhere on earth a lover of God who is always kept safe, I know nothing of it, for it was not shown to me. But this was shown: that in falling and rising again we are always kept in that same precious love.

—Julian of Norwich

CHAPTER 9

BEFORES AND AFTERS

A few weeks after we returned from Rome, my back was still fine. Miraculously, bizarrely fine. I kept going to my physiotherapist, and she kept checking all the damage points: everything was aligned; everything was where it should be. I hardly told a soul what had happened in Rome. I didn't have language for it yet; I couldn't quite understand it myself. I couldn't figure out why I was healed—why me, the skeptic, the doubter, the one who didn't need a miracle to love God? Why me—and not someone more deserving, someone who had suffered more, who needed it more, who had struggled longer, who had earned it? Why me—and to what purpose?

Coming from a charismatic background that deeply valued the abundant life we had found in Jesus—an abundance that we believed included our bodies—I had developed a complicated relationship with the God of miracles. Part of me was deeply at home with the language and instances of miracles: my childhood lungs breathed the air of God's goodness and healing power and miraculous provision. I knew people who experienced miracles themselves, and I knew them to be good, earnest, sincere people. My own father and mother had stories of God's emotional and physical healing, stories I witnessed myself and could attest as true. Before, Jesus cured cancer and straightened legs and raised the dead among us.

I even graduated from a Christian university whose televangelist founder signed off a broadcast with "Expect a miracle!" Bless it. Back then, I didn't know how to conceive of a healing that involved doctors and medicine, let alone my own participation and practices of wholeness or embodiment. Healing would always be *miraculous*.

And yet over time, I also became quietly skeptical of those who claimed miracles. I grew disillusioned with the way we chased after the miraculous, the big movement, instead of after Jesus. I remember church services where healing was spoken of as a certainty, as a formula to enact. If we believed—meaning, if we believed *right enough* or spoke with enough authority or never doubted for even a moment or worshipped until heaven came down or only confessed enough Scriptures—then it could still also happen here too. We simply needed to *expect* the bombastic, supernatural, eleventh-hour miracle because we all knew God is never late or early, only right on time.

But then as I moved into my Afters—after the unanswered prayers, after the broken hearts, after the disintegration of my formulas and rules for God—then I began to realize that we valued the victory, not the struggle. We wanted the testimony of God's faithfulness so badly that we didn't know how to engage in the work of miracles and healing. The victory either came or it didn't by God's magic—there was no middle-place theology, a theology of tension, of "yes, and" for those of us who, *yes*, believed in the supernatural and in miracles *and* needed a muscular theology of suffering and unanswered prayers.

I had a vague sense of unease with this, but it wasn't until grief and unanswered prayers moved into my own home that I began to fully understand how a theology without language for lament and sorrow was insufficient.

And I witnessed the damage inflicted on the suffering by well-meaning believers, eager to diagnose the lack of a miracle and needing to fault someone other than God.* After all, if God is no respecter of persons and God wants you healed, then if you aren't healed, it naturally follows that you must be the problem with the equation—a notion that was then and remains, in the kindest and most holy of ways, complete and utter bullshit.

I remember hearing a preacher once claim the miracle of a good parking spot. As in, she taught a church full of people how to pray for a good parking spot, how to claim it, and how to rejoice when it came. My side eye at this cannot be overestimated. If your greatest notion of suffering is having to walk a few more rows to the Target, then I think we can safely say you've lost the plot.

I always felt suspicious of leaders who acted like they were perpetually "on top looking down" or always "going from glory to glory, bless God" or whose pain was always in the past. As I matured, I began to realize that it wasn't that these folks were

---

* I wrote more about this in my book *Out of Sorts: Making Peace with an Evolving Faith* in the chapter "Signs and Wonders," if you'd like to read more about this process.

doing so much better than the rest of us or that they were more holy or more blessed or more beloved than us—they were often telling their truth as they could understand it then, or sometimes they were only telling the whole truth to their treasured few. And I get that—the whole truth often only belongs to the ones who love us best, who have earned our trust and vulnerability.

But at the same time, I don't know if we are doing folks any favors if we act like when we become Christians or when we follow Jesus, all we do is win. I think it's okay to say that we mess up, that we let people down, that we overpromise and underdeliver, that we go to therapy, that we take our meds, that we go for walks to remember everything good and true, that we're still in the midst of figuring out where God is in the middle of all this, that we're learning our capacity and God's goodness the real way: by living our lives and experiencing both victories and sorrows in the midst.

Yet after my deconstruction of what I had experienced or believed or absorbed about expecting a miraculous healing, even after I had unlearned easy answers and formulas, even then I quietly rebuilt a new small shelter for myself in the conviction that God *did* care about our bodies, that miracles *could* happen even if I didn't expect them or demand them anymore or even pray for them much. In this small shelter I built in the wilderness, between the charismatic Church and my unanswered prayers, I didn't need a miracle to know that God was real, that God was good, that wholeness is relative, that shalom includes the incarnation and the material, that we are still breathing the air of God's goodness, perhaps most especially in the desert.

The longer I oriented my life around Jesus, the less satisfied I became with the language of miracles. My deconstruction coincided with my awakening to God's heart for justice. I began to have more proximity to those who were experiencing poverty, those whose life experiences were different from my own, those who were oppressed and marginalized and despised by the powers and principalities of this world. The more time I spent with the chronically sick in mind or body, the more I resented the ones who claimed, *Poof! Everything is all better now—because Jesus!* As my story began to entwine more with systemic injustice, particularly with women in Haiti through my work with Heartline Ministries, the insufficiency of my old ideas about miracles became almost *embarrassing*. I began to witness the miracles of women's agency in birth and babies. I began to witness the miracle of women supporting and loving one another. I began to witness the miracle of midwives and of cups of cold water in the heat as women labor.

I have a friend who has lived with mental illness most of her life. She does the hard work of regularly going to her therapist, of monitoring her meds, of doing the work she needs to do, of practicing the discipline of self-regulation and self-care to keep herself healthy. I know she is a miracle. I also know she found it hurtful when someone who was well-meaning shared a book with her that was all about a woman who had depression and then one day, Jesus healed her and she didn't have sad feelings anymore. My friend was glad for the author who was healed, but she didn't find the story particularly helpful for her circumstance because, despite her faith and her prayers, my friend had not been healed in that way. What she really needed was a book with a vision for living with mental illness as a woman of faith—a vision that was lively and substantive—not another account of someone else's miracle. She needed people to stop talking about her mental illness as her enemy. It wasn't an enemy. In fact, she hadn't learned to be healthy until she welcomed her whole self—mental illness included—as a friend with whom she would learn to cooperate and receive as her whole self.

Like most of us, when I walked through my own valleys of darkness and suffering and loss, God was often revealed to me in the darkness rather than in the light. The valleys were where I became intimate with God, far more than the mountaintops.

In my Afters, I encountered the Holy Spirit more in the wilderness than in any healing revival. Jesus' tears meant something to me in those places. It's not that I didn't love laughter or find Jesus in joy; it's that I had lived in a narrative that didn't recognize God in the grief, and so when sadness or loneliness or suffering came to stay, I felt that God must have moved out of my life in order to make room for the suffering.

I'm not precious and beatific about this: suffering can be a sacrament not because it's refining on its own—suffering can also make us bitter and twisted and angry—but because it can become the sort of darkness that makes the light much more beautiful.

After all, when you are in the company of those with unanswered prayers, you learn that getting your desired outcome isn't the yardstick for holiness. The Gospel has to be true everywhere for everyone, or it isn't Gospel at all. And God doesn't only hang out with the winners; indeed, those of us whom the world will pass by are very dear to God.

I wasn't wrong before: healing is always miraculous. It's just that my idea of miracles was too narrow and restrictive. These are the miracles I used to overlook. The miracles like my father's lifesaving, completely devastating surgery or like my daughter's traumatic birth or the miracle of women praying or of compassion or of unity without conformity, of former enemies clasping hands. I began to see the miracle of the therapist, of the antidepressant, of faithful sobriety, of the doctor's diagnosis, of physiotherapy, of glorious neurodiversity, of differently abled bodies, of making friends with one's body instead of an enemy, of transformed hearts, of patience, of long walks in the morning before the moon has fully disappeared from the sky.

When we returned from Rome, we quietly told my parents and my sister, our friends and close family, about what happened in Rome. Everyone was overcome with emotion. They knew what this healing meant for us. They were as shocked as we were—shocked and thrilled. We became more at home in the miracle by telling people about it—it felt more real every time we spoke of it. I wrote it out—as I always did—and sent it to a few friends, and they responded with the same disbelief and wonder and joy that we had experienced when it happened.

With my back and hips released from torment, I experienced some physical relief for the first time in a long time.

But I ignored the nagging pain and swelling in my foot, I ignored my trembling hand, and I ignored my sleeplessness and disorientation. I ignored everything still happening in my body that didn't fit into the new narrative I was now crafting.

Then I heard back from my publisher about the book I had submitted before Rome. And the news wasn't good—my editor told me the book was overwritten, shapeless, and purposeless. Oh, she tried to be kind and encouraging: "There is a lot of fine writing here, Sarah, but . . . not . . . exactly . . . a good . . . well, it's not a good *book*, you know?" The publisher pulled it from the production schedule, sent me back to square one. And just like that, I lost two years of income.

I would like to tell you that when that verdict came, I immediately reacted with great fortitude and faith and strength of character and resolve. Instead, I'll be honest: I was surprised by the sharpness of devastation. I was humiliated and embarrassed. I was disappointed. I was angry—mostly with myself for failing. I was ashamed. I was chastened. Also, I was sad. So incredibly, unrelentingly, inescapably sad. The sadness didn't hit me like a crashing wave; it felt like I sank into sadness like a weight.

My tradition likes those who frame all of their struggles or failures or weaknesses as the Before—*Before I knew Jesus, I was a failure, I was sick, I was broke, I was purposeless, I was depressed, I was a mess. But then . . . Jesus!* All the evil and brokenness, sin and sickness, was for the Before. I was supposed to be in the After—I followed Jesus; I was practically a professional Christian, what with making a living talking and writing about how I encountered God, how I was physically healed—and yet after Rome, I found myself flat on my face, unable to even fake the rising anymore. The best I can figure is this: when my back was

MIRACLES AND OTHER REASONABLE THINGS

healed in Rome, the rest of me stretched into that left-open space and said, *Now it is my turn*. I had given so much of my energy toward managing my physical pain that I had not realized how the pain had almost functioned as a dam against the deluge of depression. Once most of the pain was gone, I sank.

I was left grasping for my place in the story: What happens when the sickness or the pain or the failure or the depression—from which we have apparently been redeemed—comes to us in our Afters? What had happened to the joy of answered prayers in Rome?

When we returned from Rome, high on my aligned spine and recalibrated hip, the rejection of my book dropped me from the cloud of unknowing back to the mud of daily life with a crash heard for weeks. I embarked on what we now refer to lovingly as My Weeks of Wallowing. I wallowed in my sadness at the rejection of the book like it was my job. I rewatched all of the *Doctor Who* canon with my two older kids. I stayed up too late in the dark alone. I spent the entire summer sprawled in my house or in the backyard with my tinies.

I quit writing every single day. I decided that two books were enough and I had nothing left to give. My career was over. I wrote drafts of e-mails canceling contracts for speaking engagements for the next year and then deleted them. I made plans to finally pursue my new career reshelving books at the library (which has secretly always been my dream job—I have a thing for library carts). I read a new novel every day. I forgot how to talk to my friends. I skipped church. I stayed home. I crawled into my emotional bunker and shut the door.

At the end of the summer, my friend Melissa gave me a lovely card. It had a picture of a unicorn on the front complete with sparkles and glitter and it said *Congratulations!* Inside, she wrote, *Congratulations on your brilliant summer of wallowing. You have done an excellent job at it. Mazel tov! It's done now.* As already noted: the best friends are equal parts hair-petting and ass-kicking.

I have been sad before in my life, of course. I have been deeply sad for long periods of time. But now I know that had been reasonable sadness: the sadness of losing a baby before birth and then another one and another and another. It had been the sadness of grief over loss. One of the great sadnesses of my life was losing church for a season. It was often expressed as anger, but underneath the anger, it was really grief: I had lost a way of understanding the world. I had lost a constant source of family and belonging.

So that was the sadness of an ordinary life, the sadness we should not try to escape from because it is the sadness that means we have been paying attention, that we have been marked, that we have loved or tried or failed or cared.

This felt different. It felt like emptiness. It felt like I had never felt anything and I would never feel anything again. I was lost even though I was right here. I wondered if my physical pain had been holding this despair at bay. Once my skeleton was healed, my soul finally was free to admit that she had taken a beating over these months as well. My spine was aligned; something else was out of joint.

There is a story in the book of Luke that caught my imagination that summer. Often the subject of artists, it is a small encounter with Jesus after his resurrection on the road to Emmaus.* Two disciples were traveling outside of Jerusalem, talking about everything that had just happened—Jesus' arrest, trial, execution, and burial. Someone curious about their conversation comes alongside of them, and they tell the stranger about what happened to Jesus. They seem wistful at times—". . . but we had hoped that he was the one who was going to redeem Israel"—before telling him that the stories told by the women who claimed to have seen Jesus alive have amazed them. The stranger then seemingly changes the subject, teaching them from the Scriptures as they travel. When the two disciples arrive at their destination, they urge the stranger to stay with them and so he does.

When the stranger sits at the table with them, he blesses and breaks the bread, then hands it to them. The story says, "then their eyes were opened and they recognized" him—it was Jesus all along. And then just as they recognize him, he disappears from their sight. The story also tells us that they said to one another, "Were not our hearts burning within us while he talked with us on the road and opened the Scriptures to us?" They return at once to the rest of the disciples in Jerusalem and tell their story of encountering the risen Jesus.

I read the story over and over again that summer of wallowing. I began to wonder if perhaps Jesus could be hiding in plain sight, walking beside me as I trudged through another day. Would I recognize Jesus only to have him disappear again?

* Luke 24:13–35.

I sat in the silence on those late nights and marveled at the patience of the Holy Spirit. I was in a place of loss and embarrassment, and yet I couldn't remember the last time I had felt so tangibly the kindness of Jesus. So it was in those long nights that I remembered how to pray.

CHAPTER 10

LEARNING TO PRAY AGAIN

Our son, Joseph, was just a small child when he first changed my entire posture toward prayer. He had a teacher that year who often used art to explore faith in the classroom. One day, she asked her students to draw a picture of prayer in order to spark a discussion of what prayer looked like to each of them and to teach them all of the ways that people can pray.

Most of the kids drew what we would all draw if asked to draw about prayer at that age, I imagine: kneeling beside their beds with clasped hands, the pastor up front at church with her hands raised up, a family gathered around the table with their heads bowed to speak a blessing over their meal. A few kids made a list of things they really wanted just in case it counted. They weren't wrong; each of them captured something about prayer, I think.

Too often, I would have drawn prayer as a code to crack or a strategy to deploy.

I've acted like there is a formula or a secret trick to prayer, a special way of praying that will ensure the results I am so certain are the right ones. After all, to my old way of thinking, the people who are mighty men and women of prayer are the ones who get results.

I could draw pictures of all the acronyms I've deployed in order to make sure I tick all the proper boxes of prayer (*A-C-T-S*: Did I remember Adoration, Confession, Thanksgiving, Supplication? Or perhaps *P-R-A-Y*: Praise, Repent, Ask, and then Yield?) lest I leave off some important step and thus render my prayer inadmissible to the Holy of Holies.

I've prayed name-it-and-claim-it prayers with great sincerity. I've quoted Bible verses at God for years at a time and called it prayer. I have made big commitments to praying in the mornings only to fall asleep five minutes in. I should probably include a picture of a clock to show how often I've checked my watch to see if I've prayed "enough"—how is it possible that it's only been fifteen minutes when I've prayed for everyone I know and through the newspaper twice?

I have always prayed in tongues. I know that is weird to some people, and I get that. It *is* weird. But who ever said that prayer, that conversations with the Eternal One, wouldn't be weird sometimes? I began speaking in tongues—unknown languages that rise from the Holy Spirit's intervention in our prayers—as a child. As I grew up, I thought I would eventually set it aside as an adult, that I would be educated out of the practice. But the funny thing is that the more I learned about God and theology and the Bible, the more I leaned into wisdom and thick books, the more robust my learning, the further I walked out into the wilderness of deconstruction, the more dependent I became on the unknowing of this prayer language. The practice of praying in tongues has often been my only way to prayer: when my heart is breaking, when I am grieving, when I am awed, when I am overwhelmed, when I am without words or answers or resolutions. When I am unable to connect with the God of my knowing, I turn to words of unknowing.

In Romans 8, the Apostle Paul writes about the future glory we have to look forward to, about how all of creation is groaning as a woman in labor to bring forth the new kingdom: "But the Holy Spirit prays for us with groanings that cannot be expressed in words. And the Father who knows all hearts knows what the Spirit is saying, for the Spirit pleads for us believers in harmony with God's own will. And we know that God causes everything to work together for the good of those who love God and are called according to his purpose . . ."* I remember when I was laboring to give birth to each of my children, how my throat was filled with these groanings and it felt like a longing of prayer, an alignment with the heart of God for life and life more abundant.

When I lost prayer altogether, it was because of my grief.

I didn't know how to pray when the answers weren't coming my way any longer. I had been taught formulas for prayer, intentions for prayer, rules for prayer. I was taught to pray like a victor, like an overcomer, like one who declares a win, who proclaims to God and the universe and the devil. Prayer had a purpose and a desired outcome.

But I was not winning, not anymore. I was broken-hearted, burned out, exhausted. I lost prayer not because of my disillu-

---

* Romans 8:26–28, NLT.

sionment and my cynicism, my grief, and my doubt; now the one-two-three acronyms seemed pointless, because what is the point of prayer if it doesn't *work*?

If I couldn't pray in the overcomer way of my previous life, now what?

And so I have walked through long droughts of prayer, years of what felt like silence from God. Then I would have drawn for my son's teacher a picture of a locked door because it felt like God was on the other side and no amount of hammering from me on the door caused it to open.

Perhaps I would leave the page blank because prayer felt like sending words into the void, into the silence, into what doesn't even exist. Prayer has been accusation and anger on my part, prayer has been pleading and begging, prayer has been me lying on the floor weeping, prayer has been washing my face and going to work anyway. Sylvia Plath once said, "I talk to God but the sky is empty."

There have been seasons when I couldn't pray, seasons when I had no desire to pray, when I wanted to pray but had no words, when prayer felt ridiculous and ineffectual; then there have been times when prayer felt like the only reasonable response to life, when prayer became as natural as breathing.

Prayer returned to me through the liturgy and through the Book of Common Prayer. This small book of prayers and liturgy became a lifeline because when I couldn't pray for myself and my own needs any longer, then I began to pray the words that the saints had prayed for centuries, the words that were being prayed worldwide alongside of me. That helped.

At night, I read to myself the words of Compline, willing the reading to become prayer someday:

Keep watch, dear Lord, with those who work, or watch, or weep this night, and give thine angels charge over those who sleep. Tend the sick, Lord Christ; give rest to the weary, bless the dying, soothe the suffering, pity the afflicted, shield the joyous; and all for your love's sake. Amen.

Prayer became less solitary and more communal through that practice. I drew comfort from the cloud of witnesses all praying these prayers together, at the same time, passing the prayers from hour to hour to one another like a torch in an Olympic relay race. I had no faith of my own, but in these prayers, I borrowed the faith of those who still believed, even if we would not meet in this life.

The words of those prayers began to shape me in a way that my own desires spoken aloud never could. I began to learn what it meant to pray, to wait, to declare, to hope again. I began to pray the Daily Hours; I still pray them with regularity. Then perhaps my picture of prayer would look like a book of prayers held in the hands of the saints, many people all praying together like we really believe that there is power in our gathering.

Here is another crayon rendering: I sit on the edge of each tiny's twin bed, one after another, and I lay the palm of my hand on their chest or on their forehead and we pray together. When they were *little* little, it was the classic "Now I lay me down to sleep, I pray the Lord my soul to keep. Angels watch me through the night and wake me with the morning's light." Around grade one, we move to the Lord's Prayer together.

Often a small hand will rest on top of my hand and a tiny will ask for me to pray for them: tests at school, friendship troubles, things they have seen on the news, the health of family members. Their worries and sorrows are dear to us both, and I pray with authority. With our youngest, I still sing lullabies.

My children are confident in my prayers, the way I am still confident in my father's prayers. For some reason, I feel safer in my father's prayers than in my own; I can see my children feel that way about me. They want me to pray for them; they want to listen to my voice speak those things that are not as they will be.

"Mum, will you pray for me?" and my answer is always *Yes, yes, of course—let me show you how to boldly approach grace and mercy as if you belong right there.*

As I have gotten older, I have relaxed into prayer. I think this began in earnest when a former pastor of ours once quipped that the same part of us that worries is the part of us that prays. I don't know about you, but I'm more than capable of worrying without ceasing, so this I can do.

It's hard to explain how constant prayer has become for me now, how conversational, and how it feels like a presence, an unbroken communion. It's less acronyms and declarations and petitions now. I am formed and re-formed by prayer—I know this. This awareness of the presence of God baptizes the everyday moments of my life now.

When the tinies were younger, I used to like to pray in the mornings by myself. Of course, they rarely cooperated with this vision. I had a houseful of morning larks who heard me turn on the kettle for tea and believed that meant it was time to hit the ground running. However, on the rare morning when I beat them all out of bed, I prayed at the kitchen table.

I often made a pot of plain black tea in the mornings. It

took all day for me to finish it, of course. My sister and I often summed up our mornings back then by how many times we had to reheat the same cup of coffee or tea: "It was a four-reheats kind of morning," one would say ruefully and the other would nod with knowing: this is life with tinies.

I still often pull my Bible and my notebook toward me when the steam from my mug curls upward to the ceiling after everyone has been dropped off at school and babysitters and I am meant to begin my day of work. When I read my Bible in these sorts of moments of quiet reflection—as opposed to my familiar grunt of wrestling and study and wrangling that I also enjoy—I often jot down verses as the Holy Spirit illuminates them to me. I can't always explain how this works, but it seems then as if when I read the Bible, certain passages of words will take on a brightness to my eyes and I know I need to write the words down.

That season of life didn't lend itself to hours of reflection and prayer: I snatched and scrabbled for the moments of peace and intentional prayer. If I had to restrict prayer to a timer and a time and one particular moment with all the stars in alignment, I would never have prayed.

One of the clearest memories of my teen years is of my father doing this exact same thing. I was once the one waking up early and wandering down the hall, coming upon him in his work clothes ready to go to the office as he sat at the table with his Bible and his notebook or planner, quietly writing down our needs and writing down Scripture to guide his prayers for us. So I still pray this way too: the words of the Bible shape my prayers and shape me.

I've been learning about ancient prayer formation, like the

Examen from the Jesuits or the Eastern Churches' Jesus Prayer or simply the Lord's Prayer from the Gospel. I like to learn about these sorts of prayers—I'm always interested in how other people talk to God, and I figure I have a lot to learn.

I confess, though, that it's hard not to have some baggage around this idea of Scripture informing my prayers. As I said, my initial understanding of prayer seemed like a Band-Aid formula: *Have a need? Apply a Bible verse! Poof! You're all better!* Not only did I abuse the Bible in this way at various points in my life, but I grapple with the likelihood that I did that to people who were suffering too. I also witnessed a lot of people abused by that practice, hurt and wounded and left wondering. If someone was hurting, the question *Did you get the Word on that?* almost felt like an accusation. If you were praying properly, then surely your prayers would be answered, right?

I'm not much for formulas or guarantees or steps or acronyms for prayer anymore. I guess I just don't see God as some benevolent or malevolent deity in the sky, granting prayers like wishes. Not anymore, anyway.

Honestly, the older I get, the fewer answers I have. And so prayer feels like a lot of listening. Even reading the Bible in the morning as I pray is just another way I'm listening: What is the Spirit saying to us? I believe prayer matters in me and through me, in the world and through the world.

I believe with all of my being that Jesus' resurrection means that God's heart is for our wholeness and our healing, for our belovedness and for our salvation, for goodness and mercy to chase after us and shape us. So I pray in that direction and trust that it is enough, that we will be shaped into

Christ's own, that our feet will find the path of peace, that our hearts will be tuned to cocreation and abundance and joy and love. I stumble over the promises of Scripture: *I believe, Lord, help my unbelief.* Sometimes it all seems too wonderful. I pray as an act of faith and surrender and an act of prophetic battle all at once.

I also pray while I work. Somehow, over the years, my ordinary work has become an embodied prayer. My hands have a tremendous amount of work to do in this season of my life: I have four tinies ranging from teenager to preschooler. And so perhaps it isn't my season for a consistent two-hour prayer session or meditation sessions, and that's okay.

I have had to learn how to pray while I washed dishes and wiped bums, while I folded laundry and pushed the playground swing, while I cooked meals and read books aloud for the fourteenth time, while I set up parental controls on the Internet browsers. I have learned to pray while I write and while I prepare sermons. I have learned to pray in lines at airports and to pray from the stage for people who don't really know me beyond the words I write and send out into the world. I pray while I'm in meetings, and I pray while I'm answering e-mails, when I'm researching and when I'm traveling.

Prayer has become a way of holding space for all that is broken in this world while my hands work toward creating a bit of cleanliness, a bit of order, a bit of beauty and life and healing around me.

I feed people, I clean, I go for walks, I gather with my people, I answer e-mails, I sing songs, and the whole time a corner of my soul is often calling out to God, waiting on God: *Strengthen us, embolden us, light our hearts on fire, show us we belong to each other, break down the barriers between us, give us eyes to see and ears to hear and hearts to understand.* I call down fire and love and justice and peace like falling stars, and I also pray for the courage to crack open my own life to receive their burning clarity.

But on that particular day, Joseph's teacher asked if she could show me Joe's drawing of prayer. When I sat down in the little elementary school chair across from her, she pulled out the picture of prayer that *he* had drawn, prayer as he understood it now, and she slid it across the little table to me. I still wasn't sure whether or not he was in trouble; her face was inscrutable.

Using markers, Joe had drawn a picture of the deck behind our house. A bright yellow sun was in the top corner of the page, straight lines from the ball of yellow to make sure we knew the sun was shining. The trees that frame our yard were there; our blue-gray house was drawn with an indigo-blue marker.

On the deck, he drew himself—brown hair sticking up like a scrub brush on top of his head, thick black-framed glasses, a red T-shirt—sitting in a chair.

Beside him was Jesus—dark brown eyes, thick brown beard, white robe with the blue sash like every children's Bible depiction of Jesus you've ever seen. (Initially I was just happy he had eschewed a blue-eyed, blond-haired Jesus—hallelujah.)

And then I saw it.

Joe and Jesus. Sitting beside each other on the back deck. Holding hands. At the bottom he wrote, "Joe and His Jesus. This is praying."

Joseph had drawn those little cartoon bubbles that you use in comic books to show that someone is speaking: in his bubble were the words "I love you, Jesus"; in Jesus' bubble were the words "I love you, Joseph." An arrow showed that they were saying those words back and forth, back and forth.

I love you, Jesus. I love you, Joseph.
I love you, Jesus. I love you, Joseph.
I love you, Jesus. I love you, Joseph.

That was it.

I raised my eyes to his teacher in disbelief, and she said, "I know. I know." Both of us had tears in our eyes. I wrote his name and the date on the back. I went home and tucked it into my keepsake box.

That summer of wallowing, I began to reorganize a closet and came across my keepsake box. I committed the cardinal sin of momentum in organizing: I sat down with a keepsake box and opened it. Photographs, letters, envelopes with locks of baby hair, and so many crumpled papers with the tinies' artwork, all precious to me. And there I found Joe's old drawing of prayer. I held it and felt the weight of this past year on me: all the prayers I had prayed, the candles I had lit in Rome, the prayers of priests, the anger, the sadness, the silence. I smoothed out the crinkles in the page and gently placed it back in the box. There is no end to what my children teach me.

Later that night, I sat on the deck in the evening air. I pulled up a chair beside me. I looked west to the mountains I can see through the trees, all the way across the river. In the sunset, they take on an otherworldly quality, as if they are faded and disappearing into the sky, shadow upon shadow. They are present, they shape our lives, and yet you could miss them at this time of the day.

I have said a lot of words to Jesus over the years; I will say a lot more as the years unfold. I will no doubt pray on stages like an old revivalist, and I will declare Bible verses. I will pray because I feel like I should, and I will pray because it's more natural than breathing. I will pray in tongues in worship and in grief. I will write out Bible verses, and I will pray the words of the ancients. I will pray spontaneously, and I will forget to pray. I will say grace around the table with my children, and I will beg for my father's life to be spared in a hospital room. I will pray for wisdom, and I will beg for a formula that works. I will scream at God, and I will give God the silent treatment. I will pray about war and famine and poverty; I will pray about a parking spot. I know this. I am still holding all of these forms of prayer within me, and I gather them all up. They are still mine.

But in this moment, after all the big prayers and the words of knowledge and the miracles and the despair of that year, I sat down. I pulled a chair next to me.

Everything was silent; even the dull quiet noise of passing cars receded from me. "I love you, Jesus," I said aloud. I paused in what no longer felt like silence. My eyes filled with tears, and my face broke into a huge smile. Love curled up around my sadness. My son had been right about the real conversation all along.

CHAPTER 11

LOVING A
BROKEN MIRACLE

*T*hen my body betrayed the miracle.

I had spent two months praising God for a miracle in Rome, grappling with my sadness, and studiously ignoring all signs pointing toward an impending crisis. But the pain was creeping back into my life. Every morning the pain scale ticked upward as I rose from my bed. At times, I couldn't walk, I could barely stand, I unfolded from a chair cautiously and painfully. For the first time since the miracles of Rome, I couldn't ignore the rest of my body anymore. I was frustratingly, heartbreakingly falling apart again.

I was struck by migraines, unable to sleep. I woke up exhausted and fell asleep in a fog. The pain moved in my body to places that hadn't even been impacted by the accident, which made no sense to me—the agony was everywhere. I became increasingly forgetful and vague. The most basic tasks of my life—cooking supper, emptying the dishwasher, cleaning the bathroom, going for a walk, staying focused while a kid went on a long, meandering explanation of Minecraft—became excruciating.

Every time I left home to preach at a conference or a church, I came home and crashed into a week of bed rest, unable to cope with my own reality. My foot continued to hobble me, and there were no answers.

I could barely bring myself to admit it to Brian or to our family and friends. After all, hadn't I been healed? Why was this happening? All the old theology I had worked to unlearn came rushing back in a flood: Maybe I had "lost" the miracle because of my unbelief? Perhaps I wasn't worthy of the real lasting miracle. What had I done wrong? Or perhaps what I had categorized as a miracle had only been temporary relief with no connection whatsoever to a miracle? Maybe there hadn't been a miracle at all?

The return of chronic pain to my life brought out my deep stubbornness. Almost the only thing that exceeds my ability to be passive-aggressive is my ability to dissociate from my body. I carried on in silence. *What pain? I'm fine, so very fine.* I didn't want to betray my new story of a miraculous ecumenical healing in Rome by admitting that I was once again sick.

I had experienced a miracle, and now it was slipping through my fingers. So I resolved to hold on tighter, to live my way into the story I desperately wanted to be true. I remembered Phil's words in the upper room across from the Vatican, how the oil had cooled and dried on my forehead in the shape of the cross, how he whispered that my miracle had been sealed in the name of Jesus. I clung to that.

❧   ❧   ❧

Brian took the three big kids camping for a few days that summer. I could no longer join them, unable to sleep anywhere but my own bed. I kept our youngest home with me, then just a wee toddler, but on their last day, I loaded her up in the minivan and drove up into the mountains to their campsite to spend the day. I was missing so much of the fun of our family these days, I couldn't bear to miss another moment. We would spend the day together, and then I would drive home with Maggie for the night.

It was nearly the end of summer, and the campsite had emptied the day before as everyone else went home to back-to-school shopping and laundry. We had the mountain lake practically to ourselves. Brian settled into his camping chair, and Maggie played in the water at his feet.

With a couple of floating toys and rafts, I slowly paddled way out to the middle of the lake with Anne, Joe, and Evelynn. It was fifty-five meters to the bottom of the lake, and the sky was endless above us; we were suspended in water together.

The wide silence of being in the world without traffic or the voices of other people settled on us. We floated on our backs, staring up. I taught them how to barely sink beneath the surface on their backs, so that it felt like they were looking up at the sky through the water, as if it was a window to a watery heaven. We splashed and laughed and hollered, they were diving deep like mermaids, capsizing each other's floats. The horseplay settled into a quiet floating in the embrace of weightlessness, letting time become meaningless for just a while.

It was in lake water that I first understood why water was a sacrament of the Church and how it was the perfect metaphor for the Holy Spirit, perhaps because it was bracing and clear, because it was dangerous and comforting, because the water required me to participate even as it held me up. Lake water has always been close to an awakening for me.

I am not an ocean girl by birthright. After all, I grew up in the prairies and the foothills of Canada. I love the ocean, but it's a new relationship. I can appreciate a pool's purpose. But by heart, I am a lake rat, a kid that grew up jumping in as soon as the ice was off on the Victoria Day long weekend, a kid that could water ski sooner than I could ride a bike. There are pictures of me strapped in the car seat in the boat, just four months old, and one of me, not quite ten, driving the boat, all skinny brown legs and arms covered with mosquito bites. My childhood was spent in the water at Last Mountain Lake in Saskatchewan. (Don't worry—I've already heard the jokes about the words *mountain* and *lake* in relation to Saskatchewan.)

Later, when we moved to Manitoba, we spent two summer holidays at a rented cottage in the Lake of the Woods in Ontario. I canoed at night, following the path of light the moon paints on water. The silence of water at night, the steady dip of a paddle, the glide of the canoe felt like an ancient ritual.

That was the first time I heard the call of a loon in the wild for myself. Her call of graceful, dignified loneliness made my lungs ache for everything lost; a universal longing for wilderness was in her voice.

I miss lakes like those out east now that we're in the west, but I've come to feel at home with the glacier-fed icy lakes of our adopted home. There is something about being near a lake with a rocky bottom surrounded by pine trees that makes my soul exhale. Cold lake water, the sound of the shore, the sway and creak of old floating piers, and enough time left over to waste a bit of it is my place of rest. The kids talk easily of God in the presence of water, weaving wonder with their laughter and play.

As we floated in the middle of the lake, I looked back to the shore and saw a young mother with a stroller and a couple of toddlers on the beach. I smiled, remembering the days before this crew went to school. These three big kids came to us in four and a half years. It felt like those days of chaos and joy, nursing and diapers, tears (sometimes mine) and Velcro shoes, were never-ending. I remember going for walks in places like this provincial park with them, just like that mother on the shore now: holding hands with two toddlers, one baby strapped to my chest in the Ergo carrier. Me, feeling like the axis upon which they spun through the world, unsure and unsteady and brave enough to try. Every person we passed would cluck and say, "Looks like you've got your hands full!" which was obviously super helpful.

I remember being that young mother looking longingly at the lonely middle of the lake as we stayed at the noisy and crowded shore together back in those days. I would have given money to someone if I could have gone swimming out to the middle of the lake. But just a few turns around the sun, and here I was, swimming in silent deep water with those babies who had inexplicably grown up on me.

A small garden snake skittered past us on the water, skating across the surface to get from one side of the lake to the other and paying us no mind. We startled and shrieked, laughed and splashed in mock panic. We peered down through the clear, cold water to our ghostly legs, fascinated as we watched them move. An eagle soared across the lake above us, swooping higher and higher, headed to the peaks.

The water gave my body relief, and I felt like their mother, their real mother, again for a few moments. The way my body had adapted, twisted, to keep myself from unfurling into pain for once relaxed in the lake. I felt like Sarah, my real self, again. I remembered what it felt like to exist without constant awareness of managing my pain, and as we languidly began to paddle ourselves back to the shore, I didn't want to get out of the water. I wanted to stay there, fully myself, fully present with my children, fully absent from the need to hide the truth of my body. It took a moment without pain for me to understand just how much my life had become dominated by pain and the coping with it.

I had been trying to get away with performative healing as I had tried to do after Maggie's birth: Look, yes, I was down but I was never out—look at how quickly I rose up again! *I've been healed, bless God, now let's go save the world.*

I ticked all the boxes in public, portrayed myself as resolutely fine, performing not only what I felt Christians expected of me but also what I expected of myself. I had wanted to have more control of my narrative of God; I wanted to get ahead of the story, to set the time lines and parameters of my own healing. But I couldn't fake my way to the narrative I wanted to believe. I couldn't heal myself. I couldn't fix myself. I couldn't rescue myself from the darkness.

∽　∽　∽

I had failed to be curious about my own healing. I had returned to a one-sided, narrow, restrictive story of miracles.

Now I knew I wanted to learn to love my broken miracle. We arrived at the shore and I stood up, water dripping from the wet hair plastered to my head, my children emerging beside me. My body was strange and foreign to me now, but I think it was at that exact moment that I opened my heart to a new narrative of healing and embodiment. I tipped my face to the sky until I felt like a woman in a poem, pausing in the midst of the rushing, for the revelation and the joy and the sorrow to gather like a constellation of freckles on my skin.

I was not fine. I had not been fine for a long time. Pretending to be fine would not magically make me fine; I couldn't out-stubborn my body. It was time for a new vision of healing, one that included my participation and honesty, my humility and my faithfulness, my openness and the truth.

If I believed, really believed, as I had always claimed, that God heals us not only with miracles but also with the miracles of medicine and therapy and community and practice, then this would be where I actually proved it.

When we try to script our own resurrections, we miss the places where God wants to surprise us with a more full, more whole expression of healing than we could ever imagine.

But first: I needed to find out what I was dealing with here. I had to stop running, turn back, and look my real life in the face at last. I would need to lie down before I even knew how to rise up. I went to Brian and gingerly sat down beside him in an empty canvas camp chair.

"I'm ready to admit that I'm not fine," I said haltingly.

He smiled sadly.

"Finally, Styles."

He reached out for my hand and held it firmly as I kept looking at the water.

I made appointments with my doctors again. Upon their examinations, I was surprised to learn that the miracle of Rome prevailed: my spine was fine; my skeleton was perfect. I shook my head in wonder at this gift, sealed in the name of Jesus by a priest. But if that wasn't the problem, then what was?

I was diagnosed with post-traumatic anxiety and depression, even as answers for the acute pain seemed absent. I was referred to specialists who cast the net wide for what I was experiencing.

One night, I arrived home later than I expected from the airport. I forget where I was—Ohio or Kentucky or Ontario perhaps. Flights were delayed as usual, and instead of arriving home at seven p.m. I was sneaking into the house at three thirty a.m. My entire body was screaming at me, I could barely take a step, and I was exhausted. Afterward, I spent a week on the couch, recovering.

When I went to my physiotherapist that week, she gently asked how much longer I was going to keep traveling for work. "Every time you start to feel better, you come back worse," she noted as she hooked up the ultrasound machines.

"I'm off to Florida next week," I said firmly. "I'll be fine. This is my work. This is what I do. I'll adjust."

The months dragged, and so did I. It felt like I was constantly fighting through wet sand—mentally and physically.

I wished whatever was happening was more obvious. I wished for a broken bone to mend or a gash to stitch instead of this invisible destruction. I prayed for clear answers. Maybe they could tell me to lose weight and do a cleanse—everyone else seemed to think that would fix everything. I lost track of the essential oils coming my way in good faith.

Eventually I was diagnosed with fibromyalgia, a condition of the central nervous system that causes widespread and highly localized pain, fatigue, aching, exhaustion, sleep trouble, and all of the other symptoms that were now a constant in my life. There were other diagnoses for particular parts of my body, but the overarching umbrella was this central nervous system condition that meant I had been disrupted and would likely never reset to original. My doctor told me that this can happen to women my age who experience significant trauma, like a car accident.

The worst news was that this was a chronic, likely lifelong condition. Oh, there was encouragement and hope: we could find a way to manage the symptoms, find a way to relieve the worst of the pain perhaps, find a way to minimize the intensity, try to find a better quality of life. But "better" isn't quite the same as "good," and I wanted good back. And yet my old life, my life without this condition, my life before the car accident, was gone.

We tried many different forms of treatment. Eventually I was prescribed medication to manage the pain on a daily basis, the depression, the pain on acute days, and so many bottles of vitamins and natural remedies. I filled the prescriptions dutifully and then I set the bottles up high in the kitchen cupboards, unopened. I couldn't bring myself to open them. I couldn't reconcile my vision of my self with those orange childproof bottles. Resentful, I left them there.

Eighteen months after the accident, we learned through a CT scan that a bone in my foot was fractured in the accident and, because it was undetectable to the X-rays, it was now broken. It had never mended and would never mend without intervention.

Let me rephrase that: for eighteen months, I walked on a badly broken foot, all the while chastising myself for not getting over it quicker. It's ridiculous. Isn't that a bit of a thing?

By the time I heard the truth about my foot, I was so tired of bad news, worn out from ridiculous scenarios, that I laughed in my doctor's face. It almost felt like good news: I'll take a broken foot any day, because that has a possibility of mending through surgery. Fibromyalgia was my new lifelong companion: I could handle a short few years of a broken foot.

One morning, after the unopened medication had been sitting in my house for a few weeks, Maggie woke up complaining about a missing blankie an hour or two before dawn. After getting her settled back into bed with the beloved blanket, I found that I could not fall back to sleep. I lay in the darkness, aware of an invitation.

I've become more uncomfortable with saying those sorts of things out loud to people over the years. Perhaps because I've seen the abuses of that sort of theology. I also know that this sense of intimate invitation I call the Spirit may also be what some people call their intuition or their true self or even just their desires.

But one thing I have noticed over the years of listening to this voice is that it often comes from *outside* of my own thinking. It feels like a phrase or a word is thrown over a waterfall into the rushing waters of my life like a life preserver thrown to someone drowning. The Holy Spirit makes herself known, and somehow I know this is the Word, the speaking of God in all of the forms God speaks, here. And often the life preserver that lands just within my reach is a word or a phrase from the Bible and it brings instant knowing to me, almost a sense of recognition, like the saving of me was right there all along. This experience doesn't happen often, so I notice it when it does.

As I lay in the darkness, the clock beside me counted the minutes. I rose up out of our bed and went into the kitchen. I turned on one lamp, which was all the light I needed. I saw myself reflected in the kitchen window—I still did not look like myself as I understood myself. I was puffy and swollen, twisted and uncomfortable, exhausted and discouraged. My focus shifted, and my face receded. There are two impossibly tall pine trees in our neighborhood that I can see from that same kitchen window; I've nicknamed them the Aunties. They stood in stark relief against the lightening sky, and at the sight of them against my own reflection, I quietly went to the minivan.

Before all of this, I used to walk in the mornings, but I can't do that anymore. I miss it profoundly, but eventually I learned that rather than sit at home, missing the world, I could just drive myself to a nearby park and gently walk to a bench to sit.

This way I can watch the light rise on a pond, even if the way I arrive there and abide there has changed. My husband has grown used to waking up to see my side of the bed empty; he knows by the time he is done with his shower, I will be back. He knows I sometimes need to start the days this way, in silence outside.

That morning, I sat, waiting for the invitation I had been sensing to materialize. As I sat on the edge of the pond near our house, the rushes waved in the breeze. The clouds wrapped around the low mountains and the power lines crossed the sky above me. A heron unfolded her wings and lifted up from the shore of gray water, gliding low.

There was no end to how I was unlearning and relearning God. This was a new welcome to the Both of God: how the Kingdom of God is both now and not yet. Because the miraculous healing in Rome was real, I knew that, but so was this moment at the pond in my own town with a lifelong diagnosis and a broken foot and depression staring me in the face.

Now instead, what I had thought was a story about a miracle in Rome was becoming also the miracle of an ordinary woman with ordinary grief and utterly ordinary suffering.

As I watched the heron move over the iron-gray water, that holy life preserver invitation word came over the waterfall to me: "As much as you are able, choose life."

There it was.

The heron landed in the tall grasses on the other side of the pond and stood quietly, patiently.

I sat with the words for a while. The phrase itself is from a story in the Old Testament when God is making a covenant with the nation of Israel. As part of the terms of the covenant, God says to the nation, ". . . I have set before you life and death, blessings and curses. Now choose life, so that you and your children may live and that you may love the Lord your God, listen to his voice, and hold fast to him."* Israel had been rescued from Egypt and finally was about to enter the Promised Land after years of wandering in the desert. Joshua is set to succeed Moses as their leader, and after the transition, Moses blesses the tribes and then dies.

Strangely, this was familiar to me because this passage had been read during our wedding as part of the sermon. There are few things modern Christians enjoy more than reading Bible verses and misapplying them to their own life out of context, I know, but this felt a bit different to me. It wasn't that I was trying to make that story fit into my life; rather, it felt like a familiar phrase that would be an invitation to me. At the cusp of a new era in Israel's life, God told them—choose life.

No matter what path I walked upon, healed or unhealed, miraculous or ordinary, the words that rose in my soul that morning—*choose life*—whispered that I may not have chosen this particular path, but I could, while walking it, choose to move toward life. I could choose to open myself to the possibilities of joy in it. I could choose to love and become reacquainted with my new body. I could be born again, all over again.

I could envision life as I believe God envisioned it— unashamed, just, merciful, loving, life-giving, beautiful, nourishing, and peaceful—and move in that direction still. The

---

* Deuteronomy 30:19–20, NIV.

miracle now would be in the agency of life, of rising and moving every day toward life instead of death. I could take the path of avoidance and numbing, of bitterness and hiding, of wallowing and anger, of stubbornness and resistance, or I could limp—sometimes literally—toward life. I opened my hands on the bench and rested in the abiding Presence of Love, always Present, as my son had taught me to pray. I love you, Jesus.

As the sun rose, I went back to the minivan and drove back home. I climbed the stairs to the kitchen. I could hear the shower running, but the kids were still asleep. I walked to my tea cupboard and, reaching up to the top shelf, I took out the medications I resented. I shook the small pills and big vitamins into the palm of my hand.

Choose life. I put the last pill on my tongue like Communion bread and pressed it to the roof of my mouth, blessed it, and swallowed. I stretched slowly in the kitchen, treating my body like a friend in need of care. I turned on the kettle for a cup of tea; the new day was stirring and I was where I belonged. To learn how to love this life, I would choose to turn toward signs of life within it.

PART IV

✺

Love wants to reach out and manhandle us,
Break all our teacup talk of God.
—Hafiz, as translated by Daniel Ladinsky

CHAPTER 12

SHE HAS
THE WHOLE WORLD
IN HER HANDS

J had first been introduced to God as the good Father.
I was introduced to God as Healer, God as Redeemer,
God as Jesus, God as Holy Spirit. But as I began to choose life, as
I began to see myself as healed even with chronic pain as a com-
panion, I began to turn again and again to God as Mother too.

I couldn't work as I used to work, but neither did I want to
sink back into another round of Weeks of Wallowing as I had
done after my book had been rejected. I knew that I needed to
look after myself as part of God's invitation to choose life, as
much as it lay within my grasp, to believe that I would be met
there with life. The times in my life when I have experienced
transformation, it has been at the intersection of my choices and
the divine, mystical stirring of the Holy Spirit. It's the dance that
changes me from the inside out—as I reach forward, I receive; as
I step back, I surrender; I'm becoming who I was meant to be all

along perhaps. In this turn of transformation now awaiting me, a transformation into the self that would be able to live in the tension of God's Both/And instead of our human need for Either/Or, I needed to figure out how to embody shalom practically.

I lost count of how many women made jokes to me about "wine time!" or "binge watch for the weekend" as a form of self-care. It's a quick laugh of solidarity, sure, but I knew that if I engaged in that version of self-care, I would self-care myself right into crisis or alcoholism or both. I already have a tendency to try to numb out in times of stress: I could use anything from food to wine to books to television to shopping. Ask my sister sometime about her secondhand anxiety from watching me in university: my final thesis was due and rather than tackle it, I read novel after novel (after novel) instead. As a steady, hard-working academic, Amanda has never recovered from watching me numb out on my looming stress. So I knew that for me, I had to envision self-care as more than a good book and a bath. Those things help in the moment; my life was more than a moment to me. I needed good paths to follow toward life, abundant life.

In the Gospel of John, Jesus heals a man born blind and the Pharisees investigate the healed man's claim. Then Jesus turns to the Pharisees and tells them a parable about a shepherd and a thief. The thief is foiled because the sheep won't follow him out of the gate—they know only the shepherd's voice. The Pharisees don't understand it, and so he tells them that he is both the gate and the shepherd. "The thief comes only to steal and kill and destroy; I have come that they may have life, and have it to the full."*

* John 10:10, NIV.

This is perhaps my mother's most beloved verse in the Bible. One translation* renders Jesus' words as "I have come that they might have life, and that they might have it more abundantly."

With the invitation to choose life still ringing in my ears, I found myself thinking of my mother's love for this line of Scripture. It deeply frames how she views God—through the lens of life. If it brings flourishing and abundance, peace and life, justice and goodness, she leaned into that as the pasture of God.

The line just before that invitation to abundant life; the one where Jesus says, "I am the Gate," strikes me now. "Anyone who goes through me will be cared for—will freely go in and out, and find pasture." It paints God as the gate to home and the gate to the wilderness or the mountain or the field that lies beyond. God as shepherd on both sides of the gate means to me that God is at home both in me and outside of me—there is a danger and wildness to God, and a calm homecoming too.

In Christ, our coming and our going is held as one experience with the divine. The notion of movement with God, of the dance going in and out is like the waves on the shore. Perhaps this means God is ocean and God is sand but also the tide pulling us between them both, and we experience the safety of the land and the danger of the open holy water.

My friend Kelly† told me to pay attention to the difference between self-care and self-comfort. I had a natural bent toward

---

* King James Version.

† Kelly Gordon is a good friend and for years now has modeled this to me. She eventually did record a podcast episode to discuss the concept with Meg Tietz of *Sorta Awesome*. It's episode 162: "Self-Care, Self-Comfort, What's Healthy, What's Not" on September 14, 2018.

indulging in self-comfort; what I needed now in this season of my life was radical self-care. Self-comfort numbs us, weakens us, hides us; it can be a soporific. But self-care awakens us, strengthens us, and emboldens us to rise.

Self-comfort wouldn't heal or help me in this new path; only the path of true self-care would help me to create shalom within my own self. I needed to go to my doctor appointments. I had to take my medications and vitamins faithfully. I had to show up for follow-up visits, I had to go to therapists, I had to explore my habits and find the trigger points of pain, I had to exercise gently, I had to submit myself to the daily hard work of incremental healing, I had to adjust my work schedule and my expectations and my crippling belief that God loves me more when I'm working hard.

As I grappled with how to begin to engage in my new normal, I realized something that the women at the retreat on the weekend of the accident had given to me was going to be key. Just before I left them for that drive, together they sang the old song "She's Got the Whole World in Her Hands."

I remembered that song and something that had been missing in my understanding of healing became clear. Perhaps self-care is simply joining with God to care for ourselves as a mother would care for us. As I walked through the gate, I discovered God's metaphor as a wise, capable, strong, patient, kind, no-nonsense, deeply loving mother. I knew so well how it felt to be mothered by my own mum. I remembered how her love made me feel grounded but also how she opened the doors for me and bade me to go further out into the world, secure in that love.

It is nice to be mothered. No wonder my own children like

it so much. Whenever my children have a fall or catch a cold, I often bundle them up into my arms and say, "Oh, you poor wee lamb." It was a joke at first—I did it with my big kids when I thought they needed an overexcess of sympathy. I always said it with a thick Scottish accent and grandiose affection, so they would laugh and cheer up. But by the time our youngest was born, it had evolved into a tender phrase (still in a terrible Scottish accent) whispered over them in times of pain or grief. While my hand smoothed their hair from a feverish forehead or when I bandaged up a knee or sat at their bedside while we debriefed a hard day, I saw how they melted and exhaled when I said, "poor wee lamb," in recognition of their suffering, how they leaned in to receive my soft warmth before they could rise again.

One day, when she was only two, Maggie fell and scraped her knee quite badly when she was out with her babysitter. When I saw her that afternoon, she turned to me, bottom lip quivering, and lifting up her pudgy arms, she said, "Mummy, please call me a poor wee lamb." There was something about the tender acknowledgment of her pain that she was craving. And in some ways, I still feel God as that mother-shepherd whispering acknowledgment of the pain just as well as the path to life.

And even so, my body sometimes requires a bit of "poor wee lamb" too. Sometimes, when I tuck my own children into bed for an evening of rest and popcorn and comic books, I sense God inviting me to that sort of rest, to remember that shalom isn't about restoring me to constant Doing and Going and Accomplishing, it's also a restoration and a healing and a reimagining of abundant life. This has taught me that we are worthy of love and care—not only for our own selves but for the sake of the world. This has been the question God has given to me as a practice of spiritual discernment during my life with chronic pain: How would God like to mother me today? If God was a strong, patient, wise, kind, no-nonsense, deeply loving mother, what would She want for me today? It's a great question to ask in prayer when I feel scattered and exhausted and empty.

Sometimes the answer has been simply: *Take a nap, child, I've got you.*

I have always loved the imagery of God as a mother in Scripture, so it's not completely out of left field for God to use a maternal image to break through in my life, to give me a path to follow toward choosing life. Most of us identify God in parental terms as a father—and that is deeply meaningful to me as well. And that has come easily to me perhaps because of my own father: his strength of character and conviction, his steadiness and masculine love, have been a foundation to my life. Knowing my own father made it easy for me to love God as father. He gave me a straight path to run on to see God as a good and loving father. But just as my own father gave me a glimpse of God's good character, so did my mother. She could not be erased from the goodness of God's expression. Her energy, her nurture, her fierce mama bear protectiveness, her joy and laughter, the ministry of her hands in my hair smoothing away the stress.

I find that the older I get, the more I care for the ones I love and for the world, the more I need *both*—I need both the energy of the mother and of the father. I need the fullness of the expression of

God, not a lopsided caricature of either. And in times of suffering or loss or exhaustion, it has turned out that I needed a mother.

As Julian of Norwich wrote, "As verily as God is our Father, verily God is our Mother."* So I began to picture that strong, wise, capable, patient, no-nonsense, deeply loving mother present in my choosing of life. After all, a peer might indulge my avoidance or self-neglect or selfishness, encourage me to do what feels good instead of what creates good.

But the sort of mother I envisioned—the way my own mum had mothered me when I was small—would make sure we ate well, drank water, went for walks, took our medication, read good books, challenged ourselves intellectually and spiritually, cared about others, managed our money responsibly, all of that good stuff. A mother who truly loved us would establish boundaries and offer wise counsel and tenderness of rest. Perhaps you picture Molly Weasley from the Harry Potter series. Or Sister Julienne from *Call the Midwife* or Marilla Cuthbert from *Anne of Green Gables* or Marmee from *Little Women*. Or maybe you'll imagine Maya Angelou in your ear whispering that when you know better, you do better. Maybe you imagine your own mum or a Sunday-school teacher or the mother of your best friend— whoever makes you feel safe and secure and cared for in your mind—and *then simply do what they say*.

I began to experience God as mother in my life. She would say, "You've had eight cups of coffee today, you have been on the computer for too long, your whole body is crying—time to shut down the laptop and get some fresh air and eat a vegetable, child."

* Julian (of Norwich), *Sixteen Revelations of Divine Love* (London: St. Clarke, 1843), 148. Originally published in 1670.

If I was pitying and selfish, I could picture Her telling me to open my eyes to the world around me. If I was overwhelmed, She held me tenderly as I wept.

If I was cranky and exhausted, I could picture Her telling me to get to bed at a reasonable time.

If I was struggling to walk or was experiencing a week of pain, She would silently hand me the phone and raise Her eyebrows until I called my physiotherapist.

If I was working as if the world was mine to save, She would remind me She has the whole world in Her hands. As my spiritual director often has to remind me, "The Kingdom of God is not in trouble."

And day by day, I strengthened. I wasn't always doing what felt good—I still despise exercise and am allergic to admitting that I am not fine—but what I was doing was slowly creating good, making room for good to flourish, planting goodness in faith for a harvest of abundance.

This kind of care awakens us to our true selves. Rather than hiding under the blankets and retreating from life, being mothered by God gave me a path to reengaging with life from a place of strength and wisdom and wholeness. This metaphor for self-care has given me a way to parent myself through this season of grief, loss, pain, and recovery.

Mothering has been my primary altar for encountering not only God but my own weakness. So embracing even the word *mothering* to describe my relationship with and the nature of my role with my children has been transformative—*mothering* as a verb always feels more tender, more loving, more relational, more familial, more warm to me. I love *mothering*. I'm not always good at parenting or discipling or raising or disciplining—but mothering is something I can get into with my whole soul.* I am not always good at mothering, and it doesn't come naturally all the time.

One part of mothering as I have experienced it, as both a receiver and as a provider, is that it isn't private, no matter how personal it is to us. Our experience being mothered by God isn't any different in that respect.

Shalom doesn't end at the false boundary of our own business: we are part of the communal renewal of all things. I am always mothering my children with an eye on who they are right now in this moment but also with an eye on what or who is waiting up ahead.

I want to raise these amazing, beautiful, frustrating children to become wise and strong, kind and generous, loving and whole individuals who love God and love their neighbors well. And just as I mother my children with that endgame in mind, I do believe the Holy Spirit mothers us with an endgame. It's not only our own wholeness, it is also for the wholeness of the world.

Because there is a lot of life on the other side of awakening. We are mothered for a purpose. We are awakened to empowerment. We are awakened to love one another as we love ourselves.

---

* Not everyone has this connection to the word *mothering*, and I recognize and honor that. It's a tender word for me because I have been mothered well. But not everyone will feel that. This metaphor won't be as meaningful for some—that's the nature of life. Not everything is for everyone. There is room for God to speak to us in so many ways and relationships and moments and words. But perhaps the image of being mothered could be redeemed for you too. If not, I pray God may give you another, better, metaphor for this kind of care and love.

CHAPTER 13

BROKEN FLOWERS

*T*hat Easter, I was on my own with the kids. Brian was out of town, visiting his family down in Omaha. Our church is almost aggressively informal, but on Easter, I do like to dress everyone up a bit. Surprisingly I overestimated how long it would take to get everyone spiffed up in their best, and we made it into the minivan early—don't let anyone tell you there aren't miracles. I even had time to stop for a quick flat white at the coffee shop and then to take the long back way to church. We still needed to stop for tulips on the way to church for our church's Easter tradition of covering the cross with flowers.

It was on an Easter Sunday seven years before that I had returned to intentional community, to embrace belonging to a particular church community again. It was due in no small part to this beautiful act of corporate worship that I was anticipating already.

On that morning, we had walked into the school gym to find a ten-foot bare wooden cross wrapped in chicken wire at the front of the room. It was hideous. "So much for Easter beauty." I shrugged and herded our two toddlers into the row of folding chairs. I was pregnant with our third then, skeptical of organized religion and distrustful of churches. It was Easter, and I had looked up churches in town because Brian wanted to take the kids to church on that day. I picked this one because they met in a school gym and I was familiar with that world, no more, no less.

At the end of the service, I watched—flabbergasted—as the entire community pulled flowers from under their chairs or from communal buckets at the doors to thread the blossoms through the chicken wire. The music was a big old dance party—children twirling, people singing, flowers everywhere. They transformed that emblem of death and torture into a living garden of life—together. I have never gotten over it.

Our small city is really just an overgrown town, surrounded by blueberry farms and chicken farms. We have three main roads of big-box stores through town, and almost all of us are less than ten minutes from rural roads. So on that Sunday, the tinies and I drove down the familiar back roads, all fronted with farms and wavy picket fences. We had big plans to grab our flowers from the unattended stands.

Local gardeners build a wooden table at the front gate to hold a few buckets of fresh-from-the-yard flowers. Some folks go the extra mile and build the stand right into the fence itself, complete with a mini awning to protect the flowers. The buckets are refilled every morning for passersby to purchase. There is always a bucket or a box on the table beside the sign that says *a toonie* a bunch*. We just pull over on the side of the road by a

---

* We call our $2 coin a "toonie." Why? Well, our $1 coin has a loon on the back, so everyone calls it a loonie. Even though the $2 coin has a polar bear on the back, we collectively call it a toonie (spelled like *loon* instead of the number *two*), and it makes zero sense, but here we are.

shelf of flowers, pick out a bouquet, drop a toonie into the box on the honor system, and carry on. There is something about one of the last on-my-honor economic systems in the world that draws me here almost weekly in the summer months. The season unfolds at these fences: first come the daffodils, then the tulips; as the summer goes on, we'll have lilacs and peonies and sweet peas and daisies and sunflowers and cosmos in those buckets.

The kids hemmed and hawed at the side of the road over what color of tulips to take to church, Maggie hollering from her car seat about her demands; they settled on a bright yellow the color of the early spring sunshine. We made it to church, and I tucked the flowers under our seats, waiting for the moment at the end when we have our big dance party and everyone covers the bare wooden cross with flowers.

Halfway through the service, Evelynn tugged on my arm, pointed at my feet, and said, "Mum, you're standing on the flowers!" Somehow when I had pulled my purse out to find a stash of grapes for our toddler to gnaw on during the sermon, I had inadvertently moved the flowers out from under the chair, and now I had them under my heels as I moved and swayed with Maggie in my arms.

I had not only stepped on them, I had utterly destroyed them. They were smeared, and the petals had been ground into the gym floor; the stems were broken, every leaf was bruised.

Evelynn's eyes were filled with tears, but thankfully a lady in front of us had brought extra flowers for just such a possibility, and she gladly handed a generous share of her own flowers back to my row of disappointed children.

As the music really took off in celebration, we all trooped up to the stage with our friends and our neighbors to weave our flowers into the chicken wire. The kids were dancing at the sides of the room. Someone released balloons and they floated around the room on the music. Everyone was clapping and singing, most of us were crying as we sang. The joy was palpable.

Eventually I went back to my seat and gathered up the broken and ruined flowers in order to throw them away on the way out. But then I looked at that cross, covered with perfect bright flowers: purples and yellows and pinks, orange and coral and white.

And I looked back down at my broken flowers.

I remembered a phrase from Isaiah: "A bruised reed he will not break, and a smoldering wick he will not snuff out."[*]

Then I began to walk back toward the cross, hands full of broken flowers.

When we have suffered, when we have been bruised and scarred, when our light has been blown out, when we are ground beneath someone else's heel, I hope to remember we belong to a God who is faithful to restore us. We aren't invisible to Jesus or embarrassing to Jesus, nor are we unwelcome.

In fact, Scripture tells us over and over that our very brokenness—our hurt, our oppression, our poverty, our sickness, our grief—makes us dear to Jesus. He is moved by compassion for us. His love never ends. His care for us is relentless. He vindicates, he brings justice, he brings healing, he inaugurates the right way of seeing creation and created and Creator.

[*] Isaiah 42:3, NIV.

This is so contrary to our Darwinian model of community wherein the strong survive. Over and over, we see that Jesus isn't about creating a high school clique or a sorority of the cream of the elite crop.

Jesus is about opening the doors to the ones we'd rather not have alongside of us. And Jesus was often hard on the religious elite, the know-it-alls. He spoke truth to power. He didn't duck from anger or from conflict—a spade was a spade to the King of Kings. But over and over, the bruised reed he would not break. The one who suffered, the one who wept, the one who was under the heel, the one who was sick, the one who was ignored or derided or disrespected or oppressed—these were the ones he gathered.

These were the ones he had in mind when Isaiah spoke of bringing forth justice. Everyone—even the bruised flowers—find their place in Jesus. And they are precious and beautiful.

For the acceptability of church or as a capitulation to culture, I know we've become pretty good at hiding our broken flowers. We're experts in hiding the damage. This is survival sometimes. The part that always makes me angry is when powerful or influential ones are doing both the grinding down of the flowers and the sweeping away of the evidence.

But Jesus is the one who comes to us, standing in the crowd with everyone else's gorgeous, ebullient flowers all around us, and he is the one who sees our damaged flowers, our bunch of grimy weeds, our dirty hands and our bent backs, and he is the one who places our flowers on the altar too.

In that noisy crowd of celebration and joy, I remembered Jesus' resurrected body, how he still bore the scars and the wounds that we inflicted upon him. How his own body is bruised and yet it is perfect, redeemed, and yet bearing the marks of what it meant to be human. How he knows what it is to live in bodies like ours. How the scars are exactly how the doors were thrown open for us.

The end of the story isn't our bruising, it is our healing.

The bruised reed is strengthened and becomes a mighty cedar; the smoldering wick becomes a roaring bonfire. The offering isn't the end, the tenderness has a purpose, the healing and wholeness means that even broken flowers become the wildflower in the desert, the faltering flame lights the world.

I thought of the people who walked with Jesus before and after the resurrection, the people of the resurrection. And that wasn't a label for the most put-together gang, the ones who had everything figured out, the ones who pretended there was no such thing as evil or injustice or suffering or brokenness.

The people of the resurrection were truth tellers, and they opened the doors to the ones the empire didn't want or value or esteem. They opened the doors for the ones thrown out and discarded by the culture, for the ones who were mocked or devalued or uncelebrated.

But more than that, they saw that they were a people of the future resurrection too: the bruised reed won't stay bruised and broken. The smoldering wick won't smoke forever. The despised will be celebrated, the last will be first, the least will be greatest, the injustice will be made right, the oppressed will be released, the captive will be set free, the dead will rise, the broken will be healed, the tears will be wiped away. Somehow, everything is made right.

On that Sunday, I carried my ruined flowers up to our community's Easter cross of triumph for all of us who have been the bruised and broken. I threaded those broken flowers among all of the bright and strong and beautiful and capable blooms. I made sure those pitiful ground-down flowers were on that cross too, for all of us who are bruised and bearing the scars still, for our world that is faltering and grieving and crying out for justice, for the ones smoldering with longing for a new day to dawn. In the welcome of the resurrection, love made room for them and, to my eye, everything was more beautiful because they were there.

"Mum, where are our broken flowers?" Evie asked as we began to leave at the end of church.

"Right where they belong," I said.

CHAPTER 14

SHALOM AND SANDSTONE

*I*t was the last day of October when I drove over Confederation Bridge to Prince Edward Island. In three days, I would lead a spiritual retreat for ministers' wives, the main reason I was there all the way across Canada on the east coast. But right now, double-double in hand, I was fulfilling a lifelong dream. Me, this island, and three days to spend as I saw fit.

The first time I read the classic book *Anne of Green Gables*, I was eight years old. I found an '80s miniseries tie-in paperback edition of the novel in my auntie's furnace room in Moose Jaw. We were there to visit my mother's sister and her family, but my glamorous older cousins were busy elsewhere, and I was bored: a book seemed a good choice. From the first sentence, I fell in love with Avonlea and with every quirky, eccentric character of L. M. Montgomery's world. As the years went by, I read every single book she had written, over and over. I grew up and navigated girlhood with Sara Stanley, Valancy Stirling, Emily Starr, and, of course, Anne. These heroines gave me a vision for girls who were smart, ambitious, curious, idealistic, and passionate.

It isn't a stretch to say those books changed my life—shaped my character, encouraged my vocation, gave me language for imagination and beauty, and gave me a center of honor and community and a few friends for my lifelong journey as an overly earnest kid becoming an overly earnest woman.

When life is rough, people often want to just go home; when my life is rough, I return home by way of Lucy Maud Montgomery's novels, since that is where I found comfort for most of my childhood and adolescence. If Brian walks into the living room and finds me curled up in the corner of the couch with *The Blue Castle* (a favorite among favorites), he knows to just make me popcorn, find me a quilt, and let me recharge until my internal storm has passed—everyone is happier that way. I reread them when I need reminding that the world isn't always a howling wilderness and that, as Emily Starr's teacher Mr. Carpenter said, pine trees are as real as pigsties.

Later, I read biographies of L. M. Montgomery, filling in the gaps in the romantic dream with the co-realities of her life of depression and an unhappy marriage, her ingrained xenophobia and lonely childhood. As an adult, I began to collect first and vintage editions of her books as I stumbled across them in thrift shops and used bookstores. I saw it as a rescue mission. I display these battered old books in our home like some women display fine china.

But this western Canadian had never been farther east than Toronto. People forget how big of a nation we are; the closest major city east of us here in Abbotsford is Calgary . . . which is more than a twelve-hour drive away. Prince Edward Island might as well have been across the ocean for all the likelihood that I would ever go there.

My work takes me to odd places. For every visit to a midsize American city with an identical big-box shopping center—saints preserve me from another Applebee's!—there is the occasional visit to New Brunswick, which is just a stone's throw from PEI.

At this time of year, the weather can be a bit dicey, ranging from a warm autumn to the first blizzard of the year. I called Parks Canada to find out if they were still open. Sure enough, several sites were closed, restaurants and attractions were shuttered, but the only one that really mattered to me—Green Gables—would be open for just one day after I could arrive on the Island. It was fate. And so I booked my plane ticket, packed my suitcase, rented a car, and reserved a room at an old inn.

My first night in Charlottetown, I slept well in an immaculate inn that had, with the exception of the washrooms, likely not been updated since 1905. The tub was inviting and the bed layered with warm duvets. I slept like a dream and breakfasted on tea and porridge before driving the highway north to Cavendish. My rental car was the only vehicle in the large parking lot at Green Gables; clearly I was the only tourist left on the North Shore, which suited me fine. After the crowds of Rome, I had learned that I enjoyed solitude more than sightseeing with groups.

I was met by Rita, a brisk tour guide decked out in Parks Canada khaki and an Anne of Green Gables boater hat with attached red braids dangling past her iron-gray perm. She handed me a map and told me to enjoy myself and that she would be around if I had any questions but wouldn't pester me: clearly a kindred spirit. Set free from the path and the schedules and the time limits, I stepped out into the land. I was working very hard to be breezy and failing utterly. I may have cried. (Okay, I cried.) I walked to the front yard and took a selfie right in front of the house before heading inside.

I wandered through the house at my leisure, snapping photos and clasping my hands at the sight of a carpetbag resting on an upright yellow chair. I came across Rita again, knitting in the kitchen, and pulled up a chair by the stove. We talked about old kitchen pantries, overly emotional tourists, and favorite knitting patterns for a while before I stepped out the back door to explore Lover's Lane. Beside the brook, there was an apple tree growing wild, her fruit long past its prime and rotting on the branch now. I walked slowly and carefully through the small wood, marveling at how it felt to be standing in a place that, for me, had until that moment only existed between the covers of a book.

I walked down the hill and into the nearby spruce grove, which had inspired the Haunted Wood. The skeletal trees creaked and groaned deliciously, sending shivers up my own spine, even though I knew better than to look for the White Lady. I emerged from the Haunted Wood to cross a road to the MacNeill Farm, where Lucy Maud had grown up. The house wasn't there any longer; only the foundation remained, but the aspect was unchanged, and I stood looking over the fields she loved and understood why she loved this place so particularly, the way I love my own place in the world, the way I have been formed by it. I tucked a few stones from the path into my jacket pocket.

Eventually I made my way to the small graveyard along the

main road. I come from a Scottish background on my mother's side, and I grinned at all of the familiar last names carved into every single stone—an entire graveyard of Scots, it seemed.

I walked up to Lucy Maud's underwhelming shared grave, carved with her married name, MacDonald, where she was identified beneath her husband's name as Lucy Maud Montgomery MacDonald, wife of Reverend Ewan MacDonald, along with only her dates of birth and death. I could see that in the summer, a flower bed would once again bloom at the base of the stone, but on this late autumn day, there was nothing to mark the grave but the bare stems.

Digging into my jacket pocket, I placed a stone from the lane near her old home at the top of her grave. "Thank you," I said quietly. "Your words mattered to me."

I was suddenly struck by the memory of the pilgrims in Rome, crossing the basilica floor on their knees, and I repented again for my pride and condescension. We are all on pilgrimage somehow.

For the next two days, I wandered on the North Shore. I made my way on back roads so that I wouldn't miss the countryside's trees turning golden and amber with the cold. I often stopped at one of the many tiny white churches dotting the landscape to stretch as I had learned to do to keep my body a bit happier. At one such stop, when I stood up straight, a beautiful red fox stood at the edge of the trees ringing the church, staring at me. The cunning fox watched me steadily as I continued to stretch out my aching limbs, and then I tipped an imaginary hat to him when I climbed back into the vehicle to carry on my journey.

I indulged every whim and fancy of my own. I listened to CBC as I puttered to see the places I knew from books and an '80s miniseries. I went to Silver Bush, and the shuttered Dalvay-by-the-Sea, and the Lake of Shining Waters, where I was unsurprised to encounter a heron standing sentry in the rushes. I spent a small fortune on yarn and tea cozies and crests at Northern Watters Knitwear before I even got to the Anne of Green Gables store in Charlottetown. I went looking for Captain Jim's Lighthouse but was unsuccessful, though I did stumble across the bright white-and-red Covehead Harbour Lighthouse, which lit up as the sun went down, the light revolving as if ships were still coming across the waters. I ate mussels and lobster drenched in butter every night without a care. I took my painkillers. I did my stretches at the churches along the road. When I was tired, I rested. When I walked, I went slowly. I even wryly deployed a cadre of essential oils.

I decided I could teach Joel Osteen a thing or two about living one's best life. I was remembering what it felt like to be at peace.

There is a vision of biblical shalom that caught my heart and mind years ago, a vision of what God dreams of for us and for the land. Though it was initially articulated to me by theologian Walter Brueggemann as "a persistent vision of joy, well-being, harmony, and prosperity," I have actually grown to love pastor and theologian Osheta Moore's explanation of shalom as "the breadth, depth, climate, and smell of the kingdom of God." She writes of shalom as "the counter-story, with nothing missing and nothing lost for everyone who reads it. . . . We, through the guidance of the Holy Spirit, catch glimpses of shalom, and pull our friends to stand in our line of vision so that they too can see the beauty of the kingdom. Shalom is what happens when the love of God meets our most tender places."*

I know that shalom is communal. That it has to happen together or not at all. We are endlessly invited into what theologian Randy S. Woodley calls "the community of creation," where we can participate fully in the life of shalom, a vision that includes not just us but the land too. Our lives become outposts of shalom, holy signs along the path giving a lost and broken and unhealthy world a glimpse of the abundant life that we have found in Jesus.

And yet for me, it's hard to remember that my own body is also included in that persistent vision of shalom. It's easy for me to see my work on behalf of *others* is part of a life of shalom.

I know I'm participating in God's vision of shalom when I'm working to help under-served women in Haiti have access to proper maternal health care. I know I'm participating in God's vision of shalom when I take my daughter to volunteer at the thrift store to dust shelves, when I'm making a meal for someone who is grieving, when I write letters or make phone calls to politicians on behalf of the vulnerable and oppressed, when I am opening the door of our home to our neighbors, when I am signing petitions, when I am learning from voices I used to ignore, when I am caring for creation as a steward, when I

* Osheta Moore, *Shalom Sistas: Living Wholeheartedly in a Brokenhearted World* (Harrisonburg, VA: Herald Press, 2017), 31.

am protesting violence, when I am one woman preaching to a roomful of men who don't believe women should be allowed to speak in church, when I am praying, when I am writing communication plans for nonprofits who serve the poor: absolutely. These are things I know and understand, things I do imperfectly and less often than I would like to admit, but still: shalom.

But to see myself—my body, as I live and move and have my being, my aching, tired, imperfectly healed body—as part of that vision of shalom was something new for me. The accident and my new relationship with my imperfect body was reawakening my longing for shalom—but this time, I wanted that to extend to my own body.

I believe God cares so deeply about this world—our material world matters to God. As Wendell Berry writes, "I take literally the statement in the Gospel of John that God loves the world. I believe that the world was created and approved by love, that it subsists, coheres, and endures by love, and that, insofar as it is redeemable, it can be redeemed only by love. I believe that divine love, incarnate and indwelling in the world, summons the world always toward wholeness, which ultimately is reconciliation and atonement with God."*

I believe we were created in the image of God, all of us, and we were all named good. The incarnation—Jesus as human—is a blessing and affirmation of these very human bodies, in all their variety. We are temples, yes, and I believe that God longed for shalom and wholeness in our material world because of that deep creative love. Being a Christian also means an embrace of

* Wendell Berry, *The Art of the Commonplace: The Agrarian Essays* (Berkeley, CA: Counterpoint, 2002), 146.

embodiment—it means dwelling fully here in this body because it is good and it is redeemed and it is central to who we are in Christ and how we know and follow Jesus.

And so this trip was not only a pilgrimage but an expression of how I was slowly becoming friends with my new body, learning to love my limitations and my changing shape in response to the new normal. I needed to embody shalom within as much as without.

Flannery O'Connor wrote, "I am always astonished at the emphasis the Church puts on the body. It is not the soul that will rise but the body, glorified." This has always astonished me too. I used to feel a guilty sort of understanding for the gnostics, those ancient thinkers who were convinced that the material, the physical, was somehow less spiritual than the intellectual or interior world, even going so far as to pit the physical against the spiritual with the results that the physical was always base and lesser. After all, how could the divine be part of *this*—our flesh, our dirt, our mess, our urges, our desires, our pain, our slobber, our curves, our hunger, our orgasms? Is my body . . . blessed? As it is, right now, *blessed*? Part of shalom's community?

This new way of being in the world as a person with chronic illness has uncovered my hidden gnosticism. I tended to live in my own head and heart a bit anyway. I never used to consider my body when I wanted to relax—I still don't understand people like my brother-in-law, Adam, who likes to go for a run to relax. To chill, I read fun books instead of serious books, or I watch television or I knit. I never considered my body when I wanted to be challenged—I couldn't understand people like my cousin Sharon, who is my age and yet participates in Ironman competitions and bikes twelve miles on a regular Wednesday. To be challenged, I pull out Dr. Soong-Chan Rah or bell hooks for a good reading session. Or I decide to save the world and so march into the social justice battles, ready to establish a bit of shalom for someone else first. Because it would be easier for me if I could forget my body or act like it didn't matter.

My body won't let me get away with secret gnosticism anymore.

My body simply never figured into my life—it was my vehicle to get from A to B, it was my house that I didn't bother to make my home, and because I was healthy and able-bodied and white, I could get away with ignoring my body more than most—an unacknowledged privilege of women like me. And yet my body is part of the shalom life. Incarnation *matters*. My body *matters*. And not just in some faraway day and time of new heaven and new earth, but here, right now.

Right from the beginning, our bodies were good too. Our bodies, ourselves, were good. There is no demarcation between the material and the spiritual; it all belongs in God. We are made in the image of God, communal by creation, and my body isn't an impediment to knowing and following and embracing God, it's part of the whole redemption. It is also redeemed, blessed by the incarnation all over again. Even my body as it now stood—both healed and unhealed—was blessed.

As I said earlier, giving birth has been my initial altar for reconciling with my body. Birth was a head-on collision between my spirit and my body, all aspects of my humanity under demand. It turned out that one of the most spiritual moments of my life was the most physical moment of my life. Those moments of corded pain and joy and helplessness and power revealed more to me about the incarnation than any book I could have read. I have been pregnant eight times, I have given birth to four children, I have lost four children before birth, and each experience tore that barrier I kept rehanging between me and the Holy of Holies from top to bottom all over again.

This is where I began to have a real glimpse of what Emmanuel (God-with-us) actually means. God is blessing our bodies as they are right in the most human moments because it's then that we embody the Gospel of *God with us*. But it was after Maggie's birth that I began to understand that there was a space between loss and joy, that life could come to us also holding the hand of pain.

Now God wasn't simply an idea or a force or a concept or a dream. No, God has a body. God fed at a woman's breast. God smiled. God learned a trade. God ate and drank and slept and walked and laughed and wept. Word made flesh, born of a woman, and it matters because the incarnation matters. All of this is good.

Even if we have strayed from the original blessing of our made-in-the-image-of-God selves, we are blessed again, redeemed, because of the incarnation of Jesus Christ, all of humanity blessed because he broke through and embodied humanity, showing us how to be truly human, all over again.

When Jesus was resurrected, he appeared in his body—a glorious, redeemed, transformed body but still a body.

The Apostle Paul blew right past our symbols and esoteric ideas when he wrote, "He will take our weak mortal bodies and change them into glorious bodies like his own, using the same power with which he will bring everything under his control."

Someday, somehow, our bodies will be like Jesus' resurrected body, transformed, no longer subject to death and to destruction. Jesus had the same body but redeemed, even bearing the scars of his horrible death. I have no idea how this works or happens, but I know this: our bodies matter. I believe I won't experience pain anymore on that day because pain isn't from God. But I might be surprised by how much a glorious body looks a lot like the body I already inhabit. The counterstory of shalom has always been waiting for me.

I have had to learn slowly and diligently to practice shalom in my body—not only for the days when I am pain-free or able to walk or a certain size or physically strong. Shalom isn't for someday when I take up less space, but right now, in this body, I am making peace while taking up the space I need. As Osheta Moore says, I am exploring what happens "when the love of God meets our most tender places."

I don't think we can ever truly love something we won't allow into our space. And so I was practicing how to let my body back into my soul space.

Barbara Brown Taylor writes, "There comes a time when it is vitally important for your spiritual health to drop your clothes, look in the mirror, and say, 'Here I am. This is the body-like-no-other that my life has shaped. I live here. This is my soul's address."

Finding my soul's address lovely again has been good work. One night while I was in Charlottetown, I ran the hot water into the tub, then I slipped into the bath and leaned back into the warmth with a sigh.

The first step to learning to love my new body was to acknowledge her at all—including when she was in pain or crying out for attention or when she looked differently than she used to look. My body is not just along for the ride but a rightful part of the story, worthy of love and care. I had to learn to notice when I was in pain, to notice when things felt good, to notice when I was hungry or thirsty, to honor what my body needed to live at peace.

I bathed my aching body gently, resting in the water. Afterward I rubbed rose-scented lotion on my skin, and every time my brain tried to find the old pathways of shame or disinterest or resentment, I made myself say, "I am making peace with this body. I bless her as my friend."

I put on my jammies and made a cup of tea at the little desk beside the cozy inn's nonworking fireplace and sat down to read my book before going to sleep. I could feel the muscles in my legs from my walk earlier in the day. I smelled like roses, and I still felt warm.

So that was a good day.

The next day, I drove out toward the Gulf of St. Lawrence. The sky above me was the bright blue of late autumn, almost cornflower blue, streaked with long, low white clouds. I walked down the winding boardwalk toward the dunes, covered with tall green sea grass, only to find that the wind was much wilder than it had seemed from the road, sweeping sand over the stairs and the path in a swirl.

I clambered down the dunes inelegantly, whipped by sand, and landed on the empty beach, bum first. I pulled my knit toque out of my jacket pocket and jammed it on my head to keep my hair out of my face and my ears from ringing with the gale.

The wind was deafening and ferocious on the empty beach as I turned to face the gulf for the first time—the waves crested white, but the water was a deep sapphire blue, crashing against the red sandstone cliffs at the other end of the beach. I stood in the wind and breathed deep. I breathed and breathed as I felt I had not drawn breath since the accident, the water and the wind cleansing me like a baptism from within. I could taste shalom now: it was fresh, wild air.

I roamed down the beach slowly, picking up the occasional seashell. I played like a child, building castles to watch the sea take them back. I traced paths in the sand. As I arrived at the red cliffs, I kneeled down to build a small cairn, stacking scattered brick-red sandstones up, one after another, until my monument was as tall as I thought it could be without toppling, and then I sat down beside it. My long hair was being lifted by the wind around my head underneath the toque, and I understood why the early Church described the infilling of the Holy Spirit as a mighty, rushing wind—I felt alive and awake.

In Psalm 73, the writer asks God, "Whom have I in heaven but you? I desire you more than anything on earth. My health may fail, and my spirit may grow weak, but God remains the strength of my heart; he is mine forever."* It comes near the end of a lament: the Psalmist knows that God is good to Israel but admits that he has lost his footing for he envies the proud who prosper in spite of their wickedness, who "seem to live such painless lives; their bodies are so healthy and strong. They don't have troubles like other people; they're not plagued with prob-

* Psalm 73:25–26, NLT.

lems like everyone else.'"* He becomes bitter and questioning of God, he asks if he has remained pure for nothing, he complains that every morning brings him pain (which sounded pretty familiar to me). He comes to realize, "Yet I still belong to you."

It reminds me of a story about Jesus as told in the book of John.† He had just concluded a teaching that was hard for the crowds around him to understand, declaring himself the Bread of Life. And many of his followers left him over it. Then Jesus turns to the few who remain and asks them, "Are you also going to leave?" But Simon Peter replies, "Lord, to whom would we go? You have the words that give eternal life. We believe, and we know you are the Holy One of God."

There's a resigned faith to both of those passages to me: a patient, less spectacular testimony perhaps in the face of questions and doubt and wonder. We miss the miracle of faithfulness, of turning toward the light again and again and again like the stubborn widow who wouldn't stop knocking at the door.

Yet I still belong to you. Where else would I go? Whom have I in heaven but you? I'm still marked by the sign of the cross and I haven't forgotten the danger of miracles.

My stubborn insistence on the goodness and abundance of God has shaped my life, and for that, I have no regrets. The way my life has been developed by what I believe and hope about Jesus is enough. Even in this, even in the unraveling and weaving and unraveling again of how I think I understand God, where else would I go? Yet I still belong to God. Whom have I in heaven but you?

* Psalm 73:4–5, NLT.
† John 6:66–69, NLT.

I still crave beauty with a bit of an edge to it. I need the loneliness to counteract the crowds, pines instead of stained glass
trees, jagged rocks as much as gentle hills, thistles and roses,
herons and eagles. I need Rome, but I also need the cliffs on
the edge of the other side of the world. I need silence and con-
templation, but I also need the homely demands of my family.
I need prayer, and I need the warmth of Brian's familiar body
curled around mine in our bed, his hand resting on my hip.

I used to think that if I were really spiritually mature, I would
lose the edge to my faith. But that shadow self remains, the imp
in the back of my mind is an old friend by now. I find God most
in that wild tang, in the sparse and open space, in the unresolved colors, even in the doubt and the uncelebrated places of
our lives often neglected by theologians and philosophers. Perhaps that's why I keep wrestling with this story of God, with the
unresolved Jesus, with the wind and fire and water of the Spirit;
there's an edge to the story, more than we acknowledge at times.
As my beloved friend Rachel Held Evans writes, "The story of
Jesus is still the story I'm willing to risk being wrong about."*
This story, the big story, is worth every risk to me.

At the end of Psalm 73, the writer says, "I have made the
Sovereign Lord my shelter."† I have always loved this image of
God as shelter, a place to make our home.

Pain and sorrow can become your second tongue, but there
are older languages to learn when the Spirit improvises hope
and grace in your life. It turns out that our mother tongue has

---

* Rachel Held Evans, *Inspired: Slaying Giants, Walking on Water, and Loving the Bible
Again* (Nelson Books: Nashville, 2018), 164.
† Psalm 73:28, NLT.

always been as universal and connective, powerful and mysterious as love.

I am still sick and I was healed and I am always being born again over and over. Perhaps shalom means holding out a hand of invitation to God's dream for us, even here.

In the months to come, I will indeed have to stop traveling for work, and I will be kept at home to heal, costing me the career I love and income in our family. I will learn the steady accumulation of devastating losses that often accompany chronic illness, one loss after another after another, each one a new reckoning of grief and a new reorientation to the discipline of joy.

I will have such a severe, disorienting panic attack in an MRI machine that afterward, I will take to my bed for a week, like a Victorian, to recover, unable to speak of it until I remember that this is the blessing of losing ourselves, of rock bottom: again, I am not in charge, and that's okay.

I will have to reckon with the truth that my youngest child may never remember me or know me as I was before this accident, when I was a mother who climbed mountains and ice-skated. That my older children will always have a demarcation in their mind of Mum Before and Mum After. That Brian will miss the old me as much as I miss her.

I will keep healing slowly, but I will not be the same as I was before—we all see that. Every time someone asks me, *How are you . . . really?* it will take everything in me not to cheerfully throw something at their head.

Eventually I will have surgery for my foot, and I will learn the patience of recovery all over again.

I will continue to negotiate my private path as someone with chronic pain and fibromyalgia. I will learn what we will come to call "the trade-off"—that when I push through to be Super Mum for Christmas, the trade-off is that I spend Boxing Day until New Year's in bed recovering. I will learn how to spend my energy, my good days, carefully, intentionally, and sometimes resentfully. I will learn that I'm not in control, not even of my own body, and that's okay. I will learn how to rest when I need to rest. I will discover the limits and drawbacks of medication and learn how to advocate for my own self.

And something in my core will be different: my body was broken and I nearly lost myself in the mending. Something about God will be reset along with my bones. I will learn what it is to be an ordinary miracle.

Because I will learn what it means to love God and to have my wildest prayers answered. And I will learn what it means to love God and to endure unanswered prayers with unexpected grace from Jesus for the suffering. I will begin to understand that healing is wider and wilder, and I will learn how to pray on the other side of a strange and painful miracle. I will learn to reimagine God yet again. I will remake myself in response to the unbecoming of God.

Perhaps someone like me would never feel fully at home in the grand cathedrals and opulent palaces; perhaps when the blood of farmers and truckers, miners and warehouse workers, is in your veins, those places are not your first cathedral. I belonged under the open sky more than at St. Peter's golden tomb. One wasn't better than the other; it was just that this—this wildness, this wind, this water, this dirt—was home, and so this is where God meets with me, where pine trees served as spires and ordinary people lay out a feast.

One of my favorite obscure lines from the Bible is hiding over in John's Gospel. At the very end of the book, he wrote, "There are so many other things Jesus did. If they were all written down, each of them, one by one, I can't imagine a world big enough to hold such a library of books." I used to marvel at those words, convinced they contained hints of miracles and signs and wonders: more eyes opened, more dead raised, more children given back to grieving mothers, more people saved, more sermons to turn the world upside down, more tormented at peace, more healing, more feedings. And that might very well be exactly what John meant.

But in that moment, in the cold wind of the eastern shores and the lonely blue of the gulf and the wide open holy spaces, I wondered if the beloved disciple was perhaps also speaking about moments like *this*, the rest of being human, the centimeter-by-centimeter prophecy of shalom. Because of breaking and mending, healing and suffering, I was learning to clasp hands with miracles as the spiritual discipline they were perhaps always meant to be: disruptive and insistent, joyful and off the path, Both/And, spiritual and physical. I built that cairn on the red shores to remember: this is how it feels to be a bit wiser, a bit wilder, a bit weirder, a bit more acquainted with my own soul, and gobsmackingly, unapologetically alive.

CHAPTER 15

ONCE AND THEN

*E*very time I build an edifice for God to live within, God transcends it while still abiding within it. This has been the story the whole way through my life; this particular story has been no different.

It is always the shore and the ocean, the gate to both home and wilderness. Just when I feel that I know who God is, God unbecomes that vision and remakes. Just when I am certain that I will always experience God in the same ways, a new path opens.

Once upon a time, I met with God in daily quiet time devotions marked by the days of the week and satin bookmarks. And then I didn't.

Once upon a time, God was a safe pasture. Then God became the gate to the wilderness and the wilderness itself as well.

Once upon a time, God was my father. Then also my mother, then my brother, then my gate, then my water, then my bread, then my truth, then my way, then my life.

Once upon a time, I loved to worship in large, crowded rooms with loud music. Then I began to hear God more clearly in the wilderness.

Once upon a time, I was suspicious of authority and establishment. Then I went to the heart of the establishment and found the undomesticated perfume of the Spirit there too.

Once upon a time, God was orderly and neat and black-and-white and logical. Then God became a gorgeous rainbow of color and surprise.

Once upon a time, I thought Jesus liked the productive ones the best. But then I learned how incredibly precious it is to walk with Jesus in the shadows and the grief and the pain and the loss, to learn the comfort of the Man of Sorrows, the mending of God in the midst of our brokenness, and what it really means to be caught up in power, power, wonder-working power.

Once upon a time, I thought Communion was a ritual. Then I encountered the Eucharist as a thin place to meet with God over and over again.

Once upon a time, I thought my path was stretching out ahead of me, straight and clear and flat. Then I turned an unexpected corner to find improvisations of faith and the power of the Holy Spirit as one part charismatic, one part catholic, soaked in doubt and reconciliation and redemption.

Once upon a time, I thought a life of faith was a life of steady foundations and stable shores. Then I heard the unmistakable loon calling me out into the waters at night.

Once upon a time, I thought I would soar on wings like eagles. Then I got down in the mud with a patient heron and decided I could abide in all three spaces, the dirt and the water and the air, always near the Source.

Once upon a time, I thought we charismatics had the monopoly on the Spirit's movement and language. Then I was prophesied over and healed through Catholics and Anglicans and Episcopalians, priests and bishops.

Once upon a time, I thought liturgy was dry and routine and empty of meaning. Then I felt more alive in the ancient prayers of the Book of Common Prayer than I had in any spontaneous prayer.

Once upon a time, I thought I would laugh every time I gave birth. Then I didn't.

Once upon a time, I thought that my father would live forever. And then I sat beside him in a hospital room while machines breathed for him and I practiced saying good-bye. I thought he would always have the answers, but then we began to learn together.

Once upon a time, I believed I could bargain with God for what I wanted in my life. Then I learned to sit with Jesus.

Once upon a time, I thought God wanted to use me. Then I learned God was already with me.

Once upon a time, I thought God preferred the holiest, the wisest, the saintliest, the most powerful, the most beautiful, the strongest. Then I learned Jesus doesn't only hang out with winners.

Once upon a time, God was a Bible as textbook. Then God became a Person and the Story.

Once upon a time, God was white and middle-class and powerful. Then God became black, became brown, became Eastern, became poor, became a refugee, became the oppressed, became the ones left outside the door.

Once upon a time, I argued and debated and fought for the truth. Then I began to live within the truth.

Once upon a time, I held on tight. Then God opened my hands.

Once upon a time, God smelled like the mountains and a glacier-fed lake. Then God began to also smell like the city and like birth and like unwashed bodies in tent cities.

Once upon a time, God tasted like strawberries from the garden and fresh-baked bread. Then God also began to taste like tikka masala and pakora, like beans and rice, like Kraft dinner and frozen pizza.

Once upon a time, God sounded like a keyboard and a tambourine. Then God sounded like the drum, like the storm, like women's voices raised in song, like a chant, like a cry, like a laugh, like thunder, like silence.

Once upon a time, I knew who I was. Then I learned who I was not.

Once upon a time, God was certainty and right answers. Then God became the questions.

Once upon a time, I believed God would heal me. Then God did.

Once upon a time, I believed God would heal me. And then God didn't.

Once upon a time, God. And then God.

BENEDICTION

Here we are again, my friend. This is the story I had to tell you, and now it is told. I am so grateful that you have trusted me with your time. But before we say good-bye, I want to do what I always do with you: I want to pray over you.

Of course, my ways of praying in these next few moments might be new to you, or my ways may be familiar to you by now.

As I write these words, I am sitting at my friend's kitchen table. The sun is out and the day is warmer than it should be, so we have the kitchen door propped wide open. My coffee has grown cold beside me because I couldn't write words fast enough. It feels as if we are here together somehow. This is the glorious mystery of time and Love, all held in Jesus.

Before you go, let me do this. Give me a minute and let me rise up from my chair and come over to you. After the accident, my friend Idelette gave me a small vial of oil. It was from a shop owner in Palestine, and on the tag she wrote in her swooping script: *She rises*.

We are rising together, rising to a restored view of God, moving to stay in the line of sight of the wild goodness of Love. So if you're okay with it, I'd like to hold one of your hands as I pray, and if I could I would touch your forehead with a dot of this oil, anointing you as we pray.

I pray for the courage to admit that you are not fine. And that when you say those words aloud that you would be met by love and care. I pray that you would remain open to participating in your own healing, even if it comes to you in ways that you resent and fear at first. Just because it's new to you doesn't mean God isn't already waiting there for you in the doctor's office, in the therapist's room, on the page, in the conversation, in the solitude. May you welcome the love of God to your most tender places.

I pray that you would stay open to the ways that God is transforming us. May you be given the gift of the gate and the shepherd, the wilderness and the pasture. And when you are in that place, I pray that, like Mary Magdalene did, you will hear Jesus say your name at the moment of your greatest despair, the moment when you believe God is dead and everything is over, because then you will lift your head and rise in hope.

My friend, may you experience curiosity about miracles and the tangible patience of the Holy Spirit, that you would receive your grief and your pain as teachers. I do pray that someday when you are given that great and terrible gift of your own rock bottom, may you learn you are not in charge and that this is okay. May you be honest about where it hurts.

Your generosity, your big heart, makes me confident to pray that you would be someone who opens up the tables and swings wide the doors. I pray that you would sit across from people you don't understand in traditions you will never personally embrace, and there discover friendship and holiness and good mischief. May you give hope to the weary around you, from your place of rest, that it is okay to catch your breath for a hot second. May you sit with the suffering and notice, in every room you inhabit, who is missing from the room. May you be given the gift of crouching down on the curb and in the alleys with the ones who can't keep up with the parades. I pray that someday you are given the gift of singing the doxology with people who mean every single word of it. May you pray the Lord's Prayer in a cacophony of languages, remembering that God listens to all of us. May you relearn old and new ways to pray. May you live within God's counterstory of shalom, in defiance of the powers and principalities of this world, prophetic in your commitment to love and life.

May you keep your feet on the ground God created and remember how it feels to worship outside of the walls. I pray that you would light your candles and become acquainted with dirty miracles. May you discern the difference between self-care and self-comfort; may you use them both wisely. And as much as you are able, may you choose life.

Even if the metaphor is difficult and foreign to you, even if there is pain before there is rest to the notion, may you experience the God who mothers, the God who fathers, and the God with us and in us and around us. May you be swept off your feet by the goodness and welcome of God, the ferocious love and friendship of Jesus, the delight and disruptions of the Holy Spirit. May you love because you were loved first. And, oh, I pray that with your whole body, you would sense it, know it, believe it, and experience it.

I pray that you would experience the Holy Spirit in ways that surprise you. That you would become acquainted with the wind and the wave, the eagle and the heron, your strength and your weakness. I pray that you would be at home, right where you are, right in this particular body.

Here's something audacious: I pray that you would experience the weirdness of the divine love in ways that leave you disoriented. I pray that you would be caught off guard when God meets you outside of the boxes you have constructed and yet remains in the places you vacated. I pray you will bless the box you once needed for God and that you will treat it tenderly even as you leave it behind you.

As you reorient to God over and over again, may you embrace the ones who were taught to distrust and be loved by ones you don't understand. May you become friends with your own limits.

May the energetic love of Jesus hold you aloft so you may catch a glimpse of ordinary love. May you find a way to laugh in your sorrow, a way to hope in grief, a way to peace in the noise, and a way to rest in the midst of upheaval.

We're about to say good-bye until next time. I pray that we would both live into the truth of God's mighty, all-encompassing love that holds our answered prayers and unanswered longings, our miracles and our brokenness, our grief and our joy, our ordinary miracles and all of those reasonable things. I pray that we would keep unlearning and relearning God in response to the never-changing, always steady, yesterday-today-and-forever love of Jesus. Come, Holy Spirit. Move, Lord.

In the name of Jesus, I seal the work that God has done in you.

You may need to remember this.

Sarah Bessey
Epiphany, 2019

ACKNOWLEDGMENTS

I am embarrassingly fortunate to be surrounded by the very best community of readers, all of whom I count as friends through the page. We've done a lot of life together over the years. Thank you from the bottom of my heart for reading, for showing up to chat in person when I was preaching or teaching in your town, for your thoughtful engagement on social media, for coming to Evolving Faith, for your prayers and support over the years, for your reviews, for the dog-eared pages and underlined passages, for your e-mails and letters. It is my joy to be alongside of you and my privilege to serve you.

Thank you to the community of Evolving Faith. When Rachel and I started this thing, we only knew that we wanted to give people hope. And now you are the ones giving me hope along with remarkable love and support and kindness. Thank you. Truly. And thank you to Jeff Chu. As we walked through the saddest and scariest thing, I'm so grateful that Rachel gave us to each other, that we have been together as we grieve. Your friendship was one of the final gifts she gave to me and I'm grateful. And to Nadia Bolz-Weber, you have been a good, faithful sister to me and to Rachel.

My particular gratitude extends to the women at the She Rises retreat: your prayers and songs and friendship were a source of healing long after we all went home from Chilliwack—particularly Idelette, Melaney, Kelley, and Kallie.

Thank you to Nicci Jordan Hubert, my editor/friend who was kind and brave enough to send me back to the drawing board. I am more grateful to you than you could ever understand for your no. You made me honor the book that wanted to be born and acted as a midwife for this weird book more than I think you know. I am grateful beyond words—and we both know that's saying something.

Thank you to Beth Adams, my original brilliant and patient executive editor, as well as Sarah Pelz, who brought this book over the finish line, and to the entire team at Howard Books, Atria, and Simon & Schuster for their support, encouragement, and excellence. Thank you for giving me the creative freedom to try something entirely different and for putting up with my love of marketing plans.

Thank you to Rachelle Gardner, my literary agent since the very beginning. I am so grateful for your wisdom and guidance and friendship.

Thank you to Jim Chaffee and the entire team at Chaffee Management for connecting me to so many people over the years and for not blinking an eye when I had to take a year off to figure out my new normal. We have walked a difficult road not only in this story but in another too, and I'm so deeply thankful for you. You are good friends.

Thank you to the Church of the past and the present and the future, all expressions and families. Thank you to the adults in our life who love and teach my children—you fill in the gaps I leave, and I'm grateful for a village like ours.

Thank you to my Somewheres, who have walked many years of faithful friendship with me. We've come a long way together, and we're still walking: I love us. If I ever need to bury a body, you're still my first call.

Thank you to Heartline Ministries Haiti, especially Troy and Tara Livesay, their family, KJ, and the rest of the board of directors. Thank you for letting me be a part of the shalom-creating we're doing in Haiti. Someone asked me what I was most proud of over the past few years, and honestly, it is being alongside of you and your work. Your theology of care reminds me that there is good work to do in the world still. Give my love to the mums breastfeeding in the postpartum room, eh?

Thank you to the fellow writers, artists, musicians, preachers, activists, and thinkers who inspire me, elevate me, push me, and challenge me. If I started listing your names, we'd be here until the Leafs win the Stanley Cup. Being part of a diverse collective of troublemakers is good for the soul.

Thanks to my A.S.S.S. Sisters (don't ask): Jen, Tara, Kristen, Jamie, and Sarah G, who daily speak truth and grace (and hilarity) into my life. You are the friends of my heart and my mind and my soul. You have walked every step of this path with me, and I'm so grateful. And, Jamison, your aunties love you. The world misses you. Thank you, Glennon, for your right words at just the right time and for your generosity of spirit.

Thank you to Sally Healy, whose constant care, steady hand,

and faithful love of our family has been a gift from God for so many years now. I never know if God brought you to us for the tinies or just for me (probably me). You'll always be part of our family—even if the tinies insist on growing up.

Thank you to "Father Matthew," "Harold," and "Theo" (not their real names), Bishop Ed Gungor, Bishop Quinton and Annie Moore, Phil, and the rest of our traveling companions in Rome. You're the best kind of holy mischief.

My deep thanks also to Pope Francis, who opened up the room to a bunch of unpredictable Pentecostal-ish Protestants with such grace and welcome: may your heart for unity be a seed planted for the entire Church. May the Spirit lead us into all truth and love.

My thanks to the medical teams—the doctors, nurses, technicians, radiologists, surgeons, physiotherapists, massage therapists, ambulance drivers, firefighters, and everyone—who have cared for me from the roadside to the hospitals and beyond since the accident. I hope the day comes when we never see each other again. But until then: thank you.

Thanks to the Bessey family, particularly my mother-in-law, Leona. Your support and commitment has never wavered over the years, and I am incredibly thankful for you.

Thank you to my sister, Amanda: someday we'll get that road trip together, but in the meantime, to be loved by you is to understand true loyalty. If I do ever end up in a cult, you're the first one who would notice, and then I know you would make me call our dad. Thanks to my brother-in-law, Adam, and my two little nieces, Ariana and Addison: I love you all.

Thank you to my parents, Dave and Joan Styles. You were the

first ones to show me that God isn't somewhere remote, above and far away, because you always walked so intimately with God in your ordinary life. Because of you, it was easy for me to take Their hand too. It was so easy to understand God as both a good father and a good mother because of you. You've cleared a path for the generations coming after us all. Thanks for insisting that I get to own my story, all of it, and for pushing me to tell it.

Thank you to my beloved children: Anne, Joseph, Evelynn, and Maggie. You're my whole heart. I know life looks different now than it used to look for us, but you have been my joy and my reason to push harder into healing. I love you. You teach me more about God than anything in this universe or beyond.

Thank you to my husband, Brian Bessey. This book, like every book I write, would literally not exist without you, in both the spiritual sense and in the very practical sense. The way that you love is why I understand marriage as sacrament. Twenty years in and your courageous goodness still amazes me. You are in every word and every page of my life. I love you.

And finally, Jesus. Jesus. Always Jesus. You opened my eyes up to all of the ways I had misunderstood God. You swept into my life with holy disruption. You are the life I am choosing, over and over again. Your ways are breath and bone to me, and I'll move anywhere to keep my eyes on you. Thank you for the unending invitations further and further out of the boat, onto the water at night. I'll do my best to keep my eyes fixed on you wherever you lead: Creator, Son, and Holy Spirit, one God and Mother of us all.

IN MEMORIAM

As I write this last-minute addition to the manuscript right before it goes to press, it has only been fifteen days since Rachel Held Evans died. Whatever I write will be imperfect—I know this—and insufficient.

When she got so sick so fast, I begged God for my friend to be healed, to be restored to her husband and her two babies, because I wanted her to raise her son and daughter, to grow old with Dan, to give the world more books. I wanted to visit her in the rolling hills of east Tennessee instead of in the random cities where we always seemed to meet and to cackle over some nonsense from Twitter as we made our plans (we still had so many plans).

Instead, I held her hand as she breathed her last and now we all have to somehow live in a world without Rachel.

In her book *Searching for Sunday*, she wrote "There is a difference between curing and healing, and I believe the church is called to the slow and difficult work of healing. We are called to enter into one another's pain, anoint it as holy, and stick around, no matter the outcome." I thought of those words in her hospital room as I prayed for a miracle I knew wasn't coming in the way that I wanted, and I realized afresh that Rachel was both a teacher and a healer.

I was blessed to be Rachel's friend for almost ten years. We experienced a lot of ordinary miracles together: welcoming babies and writing books, so much life. Her friendship made me braver, wiser, smarter, more honest, and more loving. She laid a path through the wilderness for all of us wanderers and wonderers, doubters and dreamers. She wrote, "This is what God's kingdom is like: a bunch of outcasts and oddballs gathered at a table, not because they are rich or worthy or good, but because they are hungry, because they said yes. And there's always room for more."

At our last Evolving Faith, as she preached and I sat beside her onstage (madly taking notes because, holy smokes, that woman could bring a *word*), I remember looking over at her and thinking, "God, I love being alongside her." I felt ridiculously fortunate to do good work with a good sister like her at my side. Being at her side, even to the end, is one of the greatest honors of my life.

Rachel was an uncommon soul, tender and fierce, brilliant and kind. She loved Jesus. And she loved her neighbors fully in both words and deeds. Rachel always rejected what theologians call "the myth of scarcity"—she embodied and made her home in the abundance of God. In so many ways, being loved by her, being her friend, felt miraculous.

We love you, Rachel. We miss you.

RACHEL HELD EVANS
1981–2019
Eshet chayil, woman of valor

Also by
SARAH BESSEY

70099